Why I Buy

Why I Buy
Self, Taste, and Consumer Society in America

Rami Gabriel

intellect Bristol, UK / Chicago, USA

First published in the UK in 2013 by
Intellect, The Mill, Parnall Road, Fishponds, Bristol, BS16 3JG, UK

First published in the USA in 2013 by
Intellect, The University of Chicago Press, 1427 E. 60th Street,
Chicago, IL 60637, USA

A catalogue record for this book is available from the
British Library.

Cover designer: Holly Rose
Copy-editor: MPS Technologies
Production manager: Melanie Marshall
Typesetting: Planman Technologies

ISBN 978-1-84150-645-6
EISBN: 978-1-84150-777-4

Printed and bound by Hobbs the Printers Ltd, UK

To Hani and Olfat,
For bringing us to the New World.

Table of Contents

Acknowledgments

The single name that appears on the cover of a book is a bit misleading. Rather than being considered the author of the book, it is more accurate to consider that name to represent the compiler, or lead strategist of the book, for nothing is done alone.

I have been extremely fortunate while writing this book to be a member of the Humanities, History, and Social Sciences department in the school of Liberal Arts and Sciences at Columbia College Chicago. My colleagues provided expertise, guidance, and support. Many of the fields of research I engage in in this book were fairly new to me and required reading in a number of areas within which I had little familiarity, the direction provided by my colleagues cannot be overstated, I thank them all.

Stephen T. Asma and Tom Greif in the Research Group in Mind, Science, and Culture are great friends and mentors, whose intellectual breadth, moral support, and wisdom are invaluable. The following colleagues provided expertise and insight throughout: Kim McCarthy (Psychology), Andrew Causey (Anthropology), Kate Hamerton (French History), Joan Erdman (Anthropology), Glennon Curran (Law), Teresa Prados-Torreira (American History), Julia Brock (American History), Robert Watkins (Political Science), Anthony Madrid (Poetry), Peter Khooshabeh (Psychology), Rojhat Avsar (Economics), Christena Cleveland (Psychology), Liza Oliver (Art History), Jeremy Thorpe (Theoretical Physics). Our past chairs Lisa Brock and Cadence Wynter along with Dean Deborah Holdstein provided steadfast support over the last four years. Our current chair Steven Corey provided support for this book during its final indexical stage, I thank him.

My family (and especially my mother, father, and sister Dina) have been involved throughout the process of writing this book, supplying me with translations (thank you, Gabman inc.), love, laughter, sustenance, and shelter, I thank them endlessly. Liza Oliver edited each chapter and provided outstanding advice, insight, and emotional support—I thank her. The past four years of hard work would have been intolerable without the respite and reward of music and friendship, I thank the following musicians and friends for their talent and the indelible camaraderie of trying to create something beautiful: Beau Sample, Steve Gibons, Alfonso Ponticelli, Peter Khooshabeh, Bryan Pardo, Gil Alexander, Jake Sanders. Also, the city of Chicago, its great public institutions, and its talented denizens, a blanket thank you to the best city in America.

This book began in 2007 as a paper on a panel with Andrew Causey and Bill Hayashi at the Chicago Cultural Center. It has developed into what it is today through discussion with friends and colleagues, observation, papers given at The International Interdisciplinary Social Sciences conference in Athens, Greece in 2009, University of Illinois, Carbondale in 2009, the Unitarian community in Winnetka in 2010, the popular culture association in San Antonio, TX in 2011, publication in the Journal of International Interdisciplinary Social Sciences, and, of course, reference to the mountains of knowledge compiled by other scholars. I hope that this book can be as helpful to someone as other books have been to me.

Completion of the empirical project reported in chapter six depended upon collaboration with my undergraduate mentees as part of the Undergraduate Research Mentorship Initiative. Jordan Compis was an ideal mentee; her work speaks for itself, always clear, efficient, and on time. Michael Haas was a mentee during the initial stages of the project. Roger Dimitrov provided excellent consultation on all matters statistical. The actual advertisements we analyzed were secured through the diligence and kindness of Karim Gabriel (our man in Cairo) and the Zamalek sector of the Gabriels. Many of the French advertisements were secured by Hani Elias Saba Gabriel. Dr. Mona Abaza from the Department of Sociology at American University of Cairo was a gracious resource for this chapter. Many thanks to an anonymous reviewer of the book manuscript and my ever-reliable editor Melanie Marshall at Intellect books. Thank you to Holly Rose for her collaborative spirit in building the cover of the book. And thank you to the Columbia College Chicago library for supporting my research.

Every step in the writing of this book depended upon the assistance of other people. But the mistakes, they depend solely on my oversight.

Introduction

My Self and Consumer Society

This is a book about the relationship between the self and consumer society in America. There are many books and articles that explain consumerism in the twentieth century through politics, economics, and sociology. This book is about both the psychological roots of consumer society in the self—why we buy—and the reciprocal influences between self and society.

My personal relation to these questions may shed light on the approach I ultimately take. As a disaffected teenager—especially during my ten-year sojourn in California—I conceptualized consumption as a simple and somewhat mindless activity that entailed the playing out of messages programmed into consumers by an increasingly monolithic corporate culture. I found this state of affairs to be a sad substitute for more authentic, traditional, and family-based emotional experiences. The meaning I derived from life came mostly from family, intellectual endeavors, interaction with other disaffected youths, and the joy, depth, and release of music.

My view of consumption reflected my position in society, first as a rebellious teenager and then later as a struggling graduate student living in an affluent city. During that period, I did not buy on principle because, by and large, objects did not do anything for me. I say "by and large" because there were a few things that I collected intently: books, cassettes, and CDs. Somehow, these did not seem like commodities to me, rather I thought of them as vital components of my education; for example, I just needed to know who John Coltrane was and I simply had to read the nineteenth-century nihilists for the sake of curiosity. Within the context of my life, there was something about these artists that resonated with who I was and what I cherished; these objects and the ideas within them did something for me at a deep level. Getting the new record of my favorite band was exciting, finding a used copy of a book of French poetry was exciting; these objects were not a superficial part of my life.

Looking back at the relationship I had with these objects in the context of the study of the nature of consumption I engaged in for this book, it becomes apparent to me that what was central to my acts of consumption was the meaning the objects had in my life as a part of my identity as a budding "intellectual" and musician. After contextualizing my own consumption habits with their intrinsic social meaning, it became harder to see consumption as a sad substitute for other emotional experiences, or as brainwashing by corporate monsters. I read books and studied music so that I could interact with intelligent and learned people at an appropriate level; my consumption had a social context. Once I began to appreciate this, it became easier to see how other acts of consumption could be viewed in the same light; consumption was a means of creating meaning for each consumer within his or her own social context and, in particular, in terms of his or her identity.

The key insight was that identity is tied up with society and that the society I live in is a consumer society; therefore many of the types of meaning that occupy my life are filtered through the act of consumption. This is not necessarily because the act of consumption itself is what I craved. Rather, the goods themselves have a position in the meaning I—as a defined identity, that I had a large part in creating—derived from my life within my particular social context; my identity vis-à-vis goods resided in a concordance between modes of life, modes of production, and systems of values (Rochefort, 1995).

This insight, paired with a series of reconnaissance trips to China, Turkey, India, and France, led me to a comparative understanding of consumption in general. I saw that consumption occurred in these countries within dissimilar social contexts and furthermore within different contexts of how individual citizens defined themselves. For example, China, India, and Turkey struck me as societies where the individual could not be defined outside its social community. Whereas in the United States of America and in France, individuals either were not as easily defined by their community, or made it a point to think of themselves and their actions as divorced from their immediate social surroundings, these different individual orientations have concrete practical consequences for how individuals create meaning in their lives. I also connect these comparative insights with my own upbringing in an immigrant Lebanese-Egyptian household, where the family unit is more important than any individual endeavor. This was easily comparable to the way my American and Canadian friends related to their families and the subsequent manner in which they created value in their own lives.

This exploration of other cultures in relation to consumption, as well as my readings and reflections on consumption led me to the locus of the self. The self seemed to me the meeting point of the type of society we are a part of and the types of meaning we create for ourselves.

My main motivation for writing this book was to reflect upon the self in contemporary America, on what the majority of people take to be the ultimate nature of this innermost sphere. Regardless of whether people actually seriously ponder who and what they are, their selves have a particular structure and that is what interests me. The structure itself consists of fundamental beliefs about identity and the subsequent consequences these beliefs hold for society in the form of day-to-day behavior.

I set about constructing this, so to speak, "default" model of the self in contemporary America in a number of ways: surveys of students and friends, personal reflection and intuitions, gaining a historical understanding of America and the role of the individual within it, exploring the mythologies of aspiration and success in America, analyzing the rhetoric of politicians, the legal framework, advertisements, the education system, etc.

This casual research led me to propose a tripartite model of how a majority of Americans conceptualize—or do not conceptualize—their innermost selves. Americans are, of course, not all the same. They can be distinguished on the basis of gender, ethnicity, social class, economic class, level of education, and religious affiliation. An obvious question therefore is, who are the majority of Americans that I am referring to? And how do I know this is an appropriate description? Although a nation comprises many cultures, there are unifying cultures that make it possible to discuss national identity. Some of these unifying cultures are the broad historical and economic conditions of the nation (not to mention the biological definition of the human mind). In this book I derive a "default" model of the self via these unifying cultures. Certainly, not every American will be adequately described by this model but at the same time many, if not a majority, will be able to understand and, if not see their own reflection in this characterization then at least, recognize elements of their personalities and circumstances in the "default" model I provide. For this reason, I will at times use the pronoun "we" to refer to a broad and heterogeneous set of Americans for whom interactions with consumer society are meaningful for self and identity. Correlatively, regardless of whether people actively conceptualize their selves, there is salient in each person's behavior sufficient information to infer the structure of a self.

I conceptualize the self into three characteristics: the metaphysical, the political, and the personal/practical. This model can account for the spiritual dimension of the self within the metaphysical characteristic (Chapter 1), the institutional and professional dimension of the self within the political characteristic (Chapter 2), and then the dimension of mental well-being, as well as desires and hopes, within the personal/practical characteristic (Chapter 3). These three aspects of the self are connected to acts of consumption through the concept of *taste*: how one chooses what to consume within one's given social context of identity and meaning (Chapters 3 and 4). This first part of the book comprises a partial explanation of *why we buy*, while the second part of the book is about *how we buy*.

After describing the psychological, philosophical, and historical aspects of the "default" model of the self, in the second part of the book I focus on the way the self functions in society (Chapter 4). In particular, I investigate the economic and sociological structure of society and its apparent values by analyzing one of the ways in which the economic engine of consumption is engendered, namely through the use of advertisements (Chapter 5). Finally, this model of the self in contemporary America is put in the context of the rest of the world by completing similar analyses of society, culture, and advertisements for two very different countries (Egypt and France) and using them as comparison cases for an empirical study of advertisements (Chapter 6). While the book primarily offers a description of what I argue to be the "default" model of the self in contemporary America, I take the opportunity in the conclusion of the book to voice my concerns about this model as well as to make a series of policy suggestions that describe alternative social formations that take into account the context of global relations, the principles of representative democracy, and general psychological well-being. Although what follows may be used as a textbook, it is more accurately defined as a selective analysis of the self, taste, and consumer society in America.

Chapter 1

Dualism: What I *Really* Am[1]

B eing a self does not require understanding what the self is. Being a self is automatic; it requires no effort, it is, so to speak, as natural as being your self. And what can be more effortless than that? It is for this reason that the description of the self in contemporary America delivered in this book will be obvious and at the same time, surprising. The characteristics to be described in Part One (the first three chapters) are apparent in our daily activities and are understood, if ever, as the unquestioned *way it is*. What I will argue is that the *way it is*, or as it will be referred to, the *"default" model of the self*, can be described philosophically and traced historically, even as it manifests itself in our practical day-to-day behavior. The self as we know it is very much a product of cultural, social, historical, and psychological factors. Although we observe these factors in daily life as perfectly natural, their roots are deeply enmeshed in the exigencies of the historical past and in the evolved nature of the mind. Part One presents robust explanations of three characteristics of the *"default" model of the self* in contemporary American society. They comprise the psychological roots of consumer society in the self: a significant reason *why we buy*.

To be clear, I do not think the self is fully a social construction, rather I believe the form of the self to be a collection of mental processes that are themselves products of evolution.[2] Nevertheless, I believe that the way the self is manifested in individuals depends upon sociocultural conditions. In a nutshell, my view is that it is human nature to have a self (as described in empirical psychology and evolutionary biology). However, within the limits of biology, the particulars of each self depend upon social conditions. This book describes those very conditions in contemporary America.

A proper description of the dualist aspect of the *"default" model of the self* necessitates not only philosophical historiography, but also a historical contextualization of the shifts of power and influence that led to the dominance of this particular fundamental system of belief about the nature of reality. This chapter highlights two sets of reasons why our *"default" model of the self* is metaphysically dualist; the first is philosophical and historical, and the second is psychological research on the innate belief processes of the evolved mind.

The characteristic of the self, described in this chapter, is the most taken for granted because it has been, and continues to be, steeped in the language of an esoteric philosophical analysis about the nature of reality, it is the spiritual dimension of the *"default" model of the self*. Metaphysical dualism is the claim that reality is constituted of two things (i.e. substances), and that everything in the universe, including us, consists of an admixture of these two things. Metaphysical dualism may be contrasted with metaphysical monism (i.e., the view that the universe consists of one substance), which itself can be broken down into what that substance is. In the case that the one substance is physical, we have metaphysical materialism; in the case that the one substance is nonphysical, we have metaphysical idealism. Although these options do not exhaust the possibilities as to the nature of reality, they have served as dominant approaches in the western philosophical tradition. With respect to the self, metaphysical dualism means the self is a combination of mind (or soul) and body.[3] An important tension broached in this chapter is that of the scientific metaphysical materialist approach to the nature of reality (an approach taken by most scientists), and the metaphysical dualism espoused, at least implicitly, by the majority of Americans. This spiritual dimension of the *"default" model of the self* mediates our deeper metaphysical belief structures, which are important in structuring what we think we really are and what the purpose of our existence is.

Metaphysical dualism is an essential part of western cultural heritage. It has roots in philosophical, religious, sociocultural, and, as will be argued, psychological, sources. It is because of these sources that despite the success of metaphysical materialism, as it is represented through science in so many aspects of modern life (for example, any technology generated through scientific research), metaphysical dualism remains the basis for the American's ultimate beliefs concerning the nature of reality, including what each of us is at the most fundamental level.

I. The Philosophical and Religious Roots of Dualism

The folk foundations of metaphysical dualism may reside in two consistent features in the lives of Homo sapiens since the origin of the species: dreams and observation of other people's deaths (Martin & Barresi, 2006). Both dreams and death suggest the possibility of other spheres of existence. More formally, metaphysical dualism also has a specific western philosophical lineage that we shall stroll through presently, originating in the Greek philosopher Pythagoras' interpretation of the tenets of the ancient Orphic cults and reaching right up to contemporary times.

The father of metaphysical dualism in this western philosophical tradition is Plato (428/427 BC–348/347 BC). In his *Phaedo*—a dialogue between Socrates and his students in the hours before his death—Plato presents the argument that the soul is not the same thing as the body because the wisdom of the soul is significantly different from knowledge gained through the senses. Plato claims the soul can be separated from the body; this separability makes it possible for the soul to be eternal, a quality that the body, alas, lacks. For Plato, the reasons for positing this separation—this metaphysical dualism—between the soul and the body were as follows: (a) all learning seemed to be a type of recollection such that knowledge must have existed before the body was fully formed, (b) that if everything dies then nothing would live, but things are alive and therefore something, that is, the soul, must be eternal, (c) things that are pure and made of only one material will not break up into parts, for example the soul is one thing and therefore cannot be disintegrated, whereas the body is a complicated amalgam of materials and thus breaks apart at death, (d) the soul is invisible whereas the body is visible, and (e) the soul has access to the unchanging truths of the universe like mathematics, whereas the body only grasps ephemeral sensory knowledge.

The theologian St. Augustine of Hippo (354 CE–430 CE) assimilated Plato's metaphysical dualism into official church doctrine, giving the separable portion of the human being—the soul—the further function of transcending death by surviving the body in an afterlife. In effect, St. Augustine gave official church doctrine a philosophical grounding for the notion of the soul that was further elaborated by the church fathers in the Middle Ages and now serves as the groundwork for Christianity's position on the soul (Foley, 2007).

Plato's student, Aristotle (384 BC–322 BC), the next major metaphysician in the western philosophical tradition, when exploring the nature of reality in *De Anima,* differentiated between matter, form, and the composite of both. He separated thought from perception and conceptualized the former to reside in eternity rather than in the natural world. While Plato's separable soul served as a vehicle for the transcendence of death, Aristotle's conception of the separable element of a human being, namely the ability to think and reflect (what he called *nous*), does not survive death in an individualized form. For Aristotle it is not a specific thinking being that lives on after death but rather an anonymous ability to think and reflect. This claim, along with his metaphysical monist approach to form and substance, is the reason Aristotle is not considered a metaphysical dualist. Nevertheless, the theologian Thomas Aquinas (ca. 1225–1274) and the Scholastics took Aristotle's distinction to mean that the *nous* is nonphysical and sufficiently different from the body that the former can exist without the latter. This metaphysical dualist position fulfills Aquinas' project of "faith-seeking understanding" by combining Aristotle's framework with his own need to explain how the individual soul lives on in eternity with God.[4]

Hundreds of years later, with one foot in the church and the other in the laboratory, the philosopher, mathematician, and physicist Rene Descartes (1596–1650) elaborated a clever and catchy metaphysical dualism that has since captured the imagination of many western thinkers. In the wake of the rise of empirical science, Descartes, using the painstaking method of doubt, adjusted science, religion, and folk intuition into the modern philosophical formulation of metaphysical dualism. Descartes postulated two realms of existence: *res extensa,* where the laws of the new empirical science of physics applied, and *res cogitans,* the soul's abode where the laws of science did not apply.[5] This metaphysical dualist theory posits two substances: physical and nonphysical, with only the nonphysical being a foundation for truth as demonstrated in his famous adage: *I think, therefore I am.* Descartes offers an interesting take on Plato's metaphysical dualist claim that the pure soul, made of only one material, is the eternal home of true unchanging knowledge. According to Descartes, the crucial issue of how two different substances, the mind and the body, interact is easily understood without the need for philosophy or deep meditations! This simple and somewhat flippant explanation has proven the most contentious and unsatisfactory aspect of Descartes' metaphysical dualism.[6] A few modern philosophers have attempted to update metaphysical dualism by arguing that *res cogitans* is not essentially nonphysical but may have a physical dimension (see philosophers Honderich (2004), Lowe (1993), and Popper & Eccles (1977)). In contemporary times, buoyed by the many successes of the scientific empirical approach, metaphysical materialism has become the dominant approach to viewing nature for scientists. The dominance of metaphysical materialism has banished metaphysical dualism from the desks of the majority of professional philosophers. As will be discussed, this strong philosophical rebuttal has not stopped a large proportion of the world's population from adopting metaphysical dualism. What follows is a possible explanation of why this is the case.

The success and influence of Rene Descartes' metaphysical dualism (also known as Cartesian dualism) must be understood as both a response to the historical situation of modernity, in particular the clash between science and religion, as well as an explicit formulation of our intuitive grasp of the experience of consciousness. There are two main reasons for the tenacity of Cartesian dualism, despite its disavowal by the majority of professional philosophers. The first is historical: the dominance of Christianity in western society, which holds in its belly Plato's metaphysical dualism as adapted by St. Augustine and Thomas Aquinas (among others). This philosophical foundation has made Cartesian dualism compatible with Catholic and Protestant doctrines over the course of western culture, while simultaneously serving as a spiritual response to the nascent metaphysical materialist, scientific account of the universe. As the Catholic and Protestant Churches have been a dominant cultural institution in the western hemisphere, metaphysical dualism has been deemed the orthodox metaphysical position on the nature of the self and soul. The second reason for the tenacity of Cartesian dualism in western thought, I shall argue, is psychological. Recent evidence from experimental psychology reveals that we may innately and intuitively view the world through the lens of metaphysical dualism. Before focusing on these psychological factors (section iii), let us turn to the cultural/historical reasons metaphysical dualism makes up a part of the *"default" model of the self* in contemporary American society.

II. The Historical and Sociocultural Roots of Metaphysical Dualism

The dominance of Christianity in western culture over the last two millennia ensured the inculcation of metaphysical dualism. The belief that the mind, or soul, and the body are separate substances was a cornerstone of Catholic, and subsequently Protestant, doctrine because it explained how an individual could survive death (Martin & Barresi, 2006). In response to the rise of science in the sixteenth century, the Catholic Church turned to metaphysical dualism, such as that articulated by Descartes, to preserve a space for the soul in the face of the encroachment of science's metaphysical materialist natural world of cause-and-effect laws.

While the church was, and continues to be, hugely influential to modern conceptions of the self, other social and cultural factors have also contributed to the sustained hold of metaphysical dualism. The British historian Roy Porter notes shifts in social power dynamics when alternative forms of discourse sprung up during the early secularization of society in eighteenth-century England. He suggests this led to a specific set of values in regard to metaphysical dualism. Specifically, Porter describes how a secularized British society substituted the concept of mind for the concept of soul as a secular means of maintaining metaphysical dualism. According to Porter (2003), the rise of popular print media led to a transformative period in modern identity. For example, when rags (i.e. early magazines) like *The Tatler* (the original literary and society journal founded in 1709) promoted the idea of the spectatorial man (i.e. the virtues of critically evaluating other people from the sidelines) as a progressive social presence heavily invested in self-presentation and appearance, the reading populace adopted this position in social interactions in their daily lives. The importance of the soul and the rejection of the body was one of Christianity's methods of maintaining spiritual eminence, but when the secular bourgeoisie rose in power and influence so too did the discourse of the superiority of mind (a secular concept that replaces the concept of the soul). The mind over matter/flesh debate was created and self-refinement, self-fashioning, and self-control (the virtues of the spectatorial man) became bywords for progress that replaced Christian notions of salvation. Porter recounts how this transformation occurred through the rags, the authority of medical associations, the proliferation of autobiographical writings, satire in theater productions as a play on identity, and the discourse of science in relation to the human body and the nature of the universe. That is to say, metaphysical dualism remained a widespread belief but this time in a secular context, where the mind replaced the soul.

In another elaboration of metaphysical dualism within secular society, the cultural historian Dror Wahrman's (2004) study of modern identity at the end of the eighteenth century locates a shift from identity as collective grouping, to identity as quintessential uniqueness. According to Wahrman (2004), a similar pattern of transformation was seen across England, France, and America during this time period. Wahrman claims that the collective uncertainty about identity caused by the cultural shocks of the French and American revolutionary wars, not to mention industrialization, triggered the demise of one way of understanding identity—namely, the *ancien regime* malleable masquerade of identities—and the beginning of a new, more essentialized, and interiorized regime of identity. A related element of this historical shift was the rise of the Romantic Movement, which characterized the self as psychologically deep and uniquely individual.[7] These shifts in cultural notions of the self reveal metaphysical dualism in that they demonstrate a belief in a separation between the interior mind (or soul) and the outer body. As Europe is America's sociocultural progenitor, this metaphysical dualism has consequences for the form the self subsequently took in America.[8]

So far, the historical and philosophical sources of metaphysical dualism have been discussed. But might there be something over and above society and culture—something about the way the human mind works—that makes metaphysical dualism part of the *"default" model of the self?* Recent empirical work in experimental psychology reveals that we may have an innate (i.e. inborn) tendency to intuitively see ourselves, others and the world through the lens of metaphysical dualism. It is this exciting evidence we turn to now.

III. The Psychological Bases of Metaphysical Dualism

Descartes' metaphysical dualism has been all but disproved by several philosophers.[9] The oldest and most devastating critique is that metaphysical dualists offer no convincing explanation for how the two distinct substances that constitute reality actually interact. And yet, metaphysical dualism remains the dominant belief concerning the nature of the self in contemporary American culture. This leads us to the following question: if metaphysical dualism is largely discredited in contemporary philosophy, why is it still held to be true by a large majority of society? It is as if people were holding to the belief that the Earth is the center of the universe after the discoveries of Galileo Galilei! Why do people who enjoy the fruits of a technology that is thoroughly derived from science (and ultimately metaphysical materialism) still rely upon metaphysical dualism in their dealings with other people and their ultimate beliefs about themselves? The last two sections offered philosophical and historical sociocultural reasons why metaphysical dualism is the dominant metaphysical framework in contemporary America. In this section I attempt to answer this question by summarizing recent findings in experimental psychology that suggest there is something about the natural functioning of the human mind that makes metaphysical dualism our intuitive approach to understanding the world.

The issues approached herein relate to how we know (i.e. epistemology); recent research in experimental psychology suggests that it is part of our innate human nature to have a particular epistemological position. That is, there seems to be a natural way to understand the world based on a set of innate nonreflective beliefs (see section ii) that all human beings share. What is relevant in what follows is how we think of others and ourselves, irrespective of the veridicality of these beliefs. A description of the natural processes that give rise to a metaphysical dualist outlook in the human mind is provided herein.

Let us begin with a couple of examples to demonstrate your own metaphysical dualist beliefs: when a close relative dies, does more than the presence of their body leave your life? Is it the body of your lover that so elates you, or what animates those cherished limbs? Is your pet dog's adorability due to the way it looks or do its personality and spirit play a part? For the metaphysical dualist, a relative's spirit has departed, the simple presence of the beloved is attractive, and a dog is more than its fur and spittle. These feelings are classified as metaphysical dualism insofar as they posit nonphysical entities, in these examples: spirit, presence, and personality.

There are two psychological processes relevant to metaphysical dualism in the human mind: belief-desire reasoning, and beliefs about nonphysical entities. The first will be elucidated through a selective review of developmental psychology and the second by surveying the psychology of religion and religious practices. The innate mental processes described in the next section are the basis for the reflective mental processes to be discussed in the final section.

i. Innate mental processes[10]

The field of developmental psychology investigates how children view reality. Understanding children's intuitive processes is important in gauging whether metaphysical dualism is an innate belief that all human beings share or simply a culturally elaborated system of belief.

In *Descartes' Baby* (2004), the psychologist Paul Bloom argues *essentialism*—the belief that a deeper property (an essence) ultimately defines any object perceptible to the senses—is an adaptive stance infants take to the natural world. For essentialists, physical appearance indicates an object's deeper nature, its essence. Through empirical research, Bloom offers the following evidence in favor of the idea that infants are essentialists in that they think each object has a deeper nonphysical essence: (a) nine-month-olds act as if they understand that objects of the same category share hidden properties, for example they act differently toward animate and inanimate objects, (b) children believe that if you remove the insides of a dog, it is no longer really a dog and cannot do typical dog activities; in general, children give greater weight to internal hidden properties than observable external features, and (c) only when transformations are described as changing the innards of an animal—presumably, its essence—do children, like adults, believe the type of animal has changed. Since an essence is a nonphysical property that gives any object identity, it can be considered unchanging, in contrast to physical properties, which are subject to change. For example, as we grow older we change in countless ways, but a sense of continuity persists between past and present. If, as we age, our body is not the same as it used to be, and different thoughts occupy our minds, what is it that remains the same? In this case, it seems to be our essence: our identity. This unchangeable essence is not a physical property; therefore belief in such an essence would qualify as belief in a nonphysical property, a form of metaphysical dualism.

Contrary to the blank slate doctrine (i.e. the claim that the mind is born empty), developmental psychology shows that children are born able to understand certain phenomena very easily while finding other phenomena entirely incomprehensible (Piaget, 1926). The developmental cognitive psychologist Elizabeth Spelke has studied children's *core knowledge systems* (i.e. a knowledge, or ability, that an infant possesses without having to learn) about physical objects through an ingenious experimental method predicated on the idea that three-month-old infants look longer at novel stimuli than at familiar stimuli.

Using this paradigm, Spelke and her collaborators found infants look longer at displays that break the following physical rules: cohesion (i.e. parts of a whole stay together), solidity (i.e. a solid object does not change form and cannot be intersected), continuity (i.e. an object continues even if it is occluded by another object), and contact (i.e. every action leads to a reaction). Based on these findings, Spelke infers that for infants, breaking physical rules is a novelty because these rules are innate *core knowledge systems* about the nature of physical reality. Since Spelke's research suggests infants possess inborn knowledge systems about physical reality, might they also have inborn knowledge about nonphysical mental reality? Do infants treat inanimate objects differently than they treat animate subjects? Wellman's research suggests infants are capable of discriminating between objects and humans because children have the wherewithal to conceive beliefs about the mind, for example, beliefs about beliefs. These abilities are evident in pretend play of one-and-a-half-year-olds, in fact, before the age of three, infants already have an early theory of why people act; this is evidenced in the two-year-old's simple desire psychology (for example, the proposition, "Mark ate a granny smith apple because he *wanted* to eat it"). Before the age of three, children have a plethora of experiences that may afford a conception of imagination and differences in point of view. Desire psychology has predecessors in such infant achievements as an understanding of agency (an agent is something that acts according to its own will) and the firsthand experience of perception and action (Wellman, 1990). Wellman's main evidence for inborn knowledge of mental reality in children comes from his observations of pretend play, where children actively assume what their play partner thinks and subsequently derive pleasure from subverting and manipulating those expectations. Wellman (1990) presents evidence that children conceptualize the mind as the sum of all thoughts, whereas adults conceptualize the mind as a processor, or interpreter, of information. He also provides evidence that between the ages of three and five, children begin to distinguish physical and mental events by virtue of framework ontological theories—systems of knowledge that children construct to understand what the world is and how it works—that differentiate between two different metaphysical realms. All this evidence suggests that children do in fact intuitively differentiate between physical and mental things.

For contrastive purposes, it will serve us well to consider the adult conception of the mind. Wellman (1990) describes the commonsense adult understanding of the mental realm as consisting of several basic beliefs: thoughts are not things, beliefs do not necessarily accord with reality, desires do not necessarily accord with outcomes, fantasy is not the same as reality, mind is private and individual, mind is not body, and reasoning about the mind is different from reasoning about the body. Wellman examined whether children share these fundamental assumptions. From experiments on the manner in which children explain events, he found that children's commonsense psychological reasoning rests on a belief-desire construal of action; that is to say, children consistently locate the reasons for human behavior in what an agent desires and believes. This type of reasoning is depicted in Figure 1.1 (from Wellman & Bartsch, 1988).

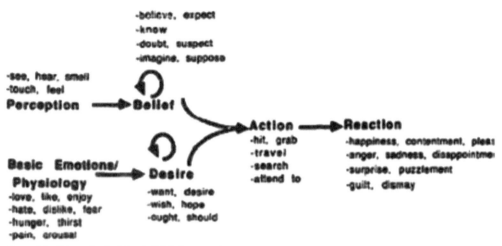

Figure 1.1: *Scheme for depicting belief-desire reasoning.*

According to the diagram, children use perceptual input to create beliefs, expectations and knowledge. At the same time, they create desires and hopes from their emotions and physiological needs. In combination, these factors lead to actions and further reactions. Such a mental scheme rests upon metaphysical dualism.

The philosopher Daniel Dennett highlights three stances we can quote while trying to explain the behavior of an object: the physical stance—the object acts based simply on physical principles; the design stance—the object acts based on how it was designed to act; and the intentional stance—the object acts based on the intentions and belief-desire contents of its mind. Humans take different attitudes to different objects—for example, when approaching a computer we feel free to touch it anywhere we want, whereas with humans we respect appropriate rules of interaction. We treat things differently depending on what we think they are. The best stance for the task at hand is the one that generates the most accurate predictions of future behavior. The intentional stance allows us to explain behavior as goal-directed by a belief-desire reasoning agent. Children, according to Wellman's (1990) research, adopt the intentional stance when interacting with other people.

This brief overview of findings from developmental psychology indicates that children possess knowledge of the distinction between mental and physical substances and the different kinds of reasoning that apply to the two substances; children seem to think differently about social agents versus inanimate objects. The propensity of children to differentiate between things that have minds and things that do not have minds provides strong evidence that humans are born with tendencies toward metaphysical dualism. But what are the specific differences between the mental processes of adults and children? Are our basic categories for understanding and interacting with the world created in childhood or do they unfurl at a later developmental stage? For the answer to these questions let us turn to research on a task that children prior to the age of four demonstrate an inability to complete correctly.

Theory of Mind

The *false-belief task* experiment requires one to attribute a false belief to another person, that is, she must assume that another person does not know something the participant herself knows. Children under the age of four consistently fail the *false-belief task* experiment; they are unable to assume that another person does not know something that they themselves know. This experimental result suggests children prior to the age of four have not yet acquired a Theory of Mind (TOM): an understanding that other people have minds. TOM is the ability of a person to impute mental states to her self and to others and to predict behavior on the basis of such states; it is the ability to take the intentional stance toward others (Leslie, 1987). The false-belief task is more complex than simple pretense, which children indulge in through pretend play, since it requires the additional step of separating what the other person believes about a situation from what that person will do. According to developmental psychologist Alan Leslie, a rudimentary form of TOM appears in the second year of life and accounts for the emergence of pretend play; it necessitates the capacity to think about thoughts (Baron-Cohen, Leslie, & Frith, 1985). This entails the ability to step back from what you believe and represent that belief as a thought capable of introspection. This meta-representational ability is necessary for TOM given the nature of belief and desire, which are personal stances toward the world that may or may not be true.

From this set of experimental results and interpretations, for our purposes let us highlight the following: appropriate social behavior requires TOM because the mind is a unique phenomenon and requires a significantly different type of reasoning than physical objects, TOM is the mechanism by which humans are able to think of others as possessing minds that contain beliefs and desires, which are the causes of their behavior, and TOM is a part of the *core knowledge system* for understanding nonphysical phenomena.

In summary, humans are born and seem to grow into certain mind processes at specified developmental stages. These stages make them see the world through the prism of metaphysical dualism.[11] Specifically, *essentialism* develops at around nine months. Belief-desire reasoning, that is the intentional stance, and TOM, are all developed at around age four. These genetically-programmed mental systems make metaphysical dualist beliefs about the self and others an innate function of the human mind. That is, if infants possess these metaphysical dualist beliefs then adult minds, built atop and through these structures, do as well. The psychological trait of metaphysical dualism in children is an element of the *"default" model of the self.*

ii. Reflective mental processes

These innate mental processes that make us metaphysical dualists make it seem intuitive as well. We are metaphysical dualists in regard to others because of the ways in which we know ourselves. Our lives seem to take place "out there," where our actions are public, and "in here," where our thoughts are private. Thoughts, feelings and our inner monologue seem to take place in a private conscious world markedly distinct from the unconscious world of dreamless sleep and the outside world of physical happenings. This is the inescapable world of sentience. The way we learn our needs and desires is by experiencing them either through feelings or reflection. For example, my leg might be bleeding, but not until I feel pain will I know that I am hurt. For each one of us, the world seems intuitively to have a dual nature: things happen inside and outside.

Perhaps we are metaphysical dualists in regard to others because we are metaphysical dualists in regard to ourselves, and we do not know any other way to be. Maybe when we encounter other people we perceive that they are human by their exterior and then by virtue of being in the same species we infer that they share the same essence, namely the metaphysical dual nature of outer body and interior mind? In *Nature's Psychologist* (1984), the philosopher Nicholas Humphrey argues for this position by describing how and why the human mind evolved to be metaphysically dualist. He explains that introspection makes it possible for us to develop a model of the behavior of others by drawing an analogy to our own case; introspection provides insider knowledge about behavior. Humphrey claims the presence or absence of consciousness in a species ultimately depends on its social needs:

> The advantage to an animal of being conscious lies in the purely private use it makes of conscious experience as a means of developing a conceptual framework which helps it to model another animal's behavior. It need make no difference at all whether the other animal is actually experiencing the feelings with which it is being credited; all that matters is that its behavior should be understandable on the assumption that such feelings provide the reasons for its actions.
>
> (Humphrey, 1984, p. 35)

This evolutionary "nature's psychologist" explanation of why we are metaphysical dualists requires reflection, while the earlier account given about the dualist innate processes of the human child does not require reflection because they are built into our genes by physical and cultural evolution. The key distinction is that the latter explanation of metaphysical dualism suggests it is an automatic feature of human thought whereas the former relies on reflective thought and intuition. The two are certainly related in that any reflective mental process depends upon and is built atop innate mental processes, including those that are non-reflective. Let us investigate this relationship between reflective mental processes and beliefs a little more closely through the phenomena of religion as it pertains to metaphysical dualism.

The Psychology of Religion
One of the unique cultural manifestations of human beings is religion, the systematic organization of beliefs about nonphysical entities. A large portion of this chapter has already been devoted to examining the historical role of religion in the creation and maintenance of a metaphysical dualist perspective. This section will go a step further by reviewing empirical

research that shows how psychological factors (innate mental processes), in their turn, engender reflective religious belief.

In the last 20 years, there has been a surge of research on the possibility that religion is an innate process of the human mind (see, among others, Humphrey, 1994; Tremlin, 2006; Bering, 2002). One of the most interesting points raised by this research is the observation that divinities generally assume a human face. The human proclivity to apply human traits to non-human things (referred to as *anthropomorphism*) is evident in the following: "Is your cat happy? Is the weather frowning down upon you? Does God understand your problems?" These common thoughts foist human attributes upon non-human objects. Anthropomorphism stems from our tendency to understand other things through the lens of metaphysical dualism, that is, in addition to seeing human agents as possessing minds, we attribute minds to all of nature. A related religious activity that betrays our metaphysical dualist nature is the importance we attach to dead bodies and the burial rituals we enact. These activities suggest that in life as well as in death, humans are more than their bodies.

For the religious studies scholar Todd Tremlin (2006), the psychological origins of religion are two innate processes of the mind that attribute human characteristics to non-human things, they are the process by which the mind differentiates agents from inanimate objects, Agency Detection Device (ADD), and the process by which the mind imputes beliefs and desires, TOM. Both ADD and TOM are innate, rapid, and automatic. These two processes allow us to function in our normal social environment by detecting what is and what is not an agent, and then taking the intentional stance to reason about the actions a given agent or object makes. Many experiments (the classic being Heider & Simmel, 1944) show that we are quick to over-attribute agency, even to obviously inanimate objects. In addition, TOM is notoriously over-active: as demonstrated in our automatic search for mental reasons behind the actions of others and our treatment of inanimate objects as if they had minds (i.e. taking the intentional stance toward inanimate objects). Religion, for Tremlin (2006), is simply an overapplication of ADD and TOM, with a dash of anthropomorphism thrown in; that is to say, it is the human way of seeing other humans applied (or rather, misapplied) to the universe. Whether or not the urge to religious practices can be completely explained by the misapplication of innate mental processes developed for social purposes is a question for further research. The finding relevant for us is that humans demonstrate a tendency toward religious thought that portrays the world in a metaphysical dualist garb, and this seems to be caused by our innate and intuitive mental processes.

The tendency for humans to approach the world from the position of metaphysical dualism appears to be the product of evolutionary social needs. But what *kind* of belief is metaphysical dualism? The anthropologist Justin Barrett (2004) delineates two types of beliefs: *reflective beliefs*, which are those we arrive at through conscious, deliberate contemplation and *non-reflective beliefs*, which come automatically and require no careful rumination. The latter are generated in each and every mundane moment while the former only surface when a conscious decision or judgment has to be made. The two types of belief are related in the following ways: non-reflective beliefs are the default of reflective beliefs;

reflective beliefs that accord with non-reflective beliefs seem more plausible and non-reflective beliefs shape experiences and memories for experiences. The two psychological reasons I have given for why we are metaphysical dualists map onto the two types of beliefs: belief-desire reasoning—which in this case includes ADD, TOM, *essentialism* and the Intentional Stance—is automatic and *nonreflective*, while the psychological factors behind religion and "nature's psychologist" are *reflective*.[12] The deep complexity of human metaphysical dualism, in the form of religious behavior, seems to derive from our ability to reason and reflect on abstract ideas and interpret events in terms of elaborate ontological frameworks. A possible cause of this ability to relate happenings in the world to metaphysical dualist systems is the Left Hemisphere Interpreter (Gazzaniga, 1999). The Left Hemisphere Interpreter is a process hypothesized to exist in the left hemisphere of the brain, which creates a cohesive narrative from our experiences.[13] The Left Hemisphere Interpreter appears to make "sense" of whatever information it is given in the form of a fabricated story. Some researchers claim the Left Hemisphere Interpreter is implicated in the construction of our own autobiography from our disparate memories; that the Interpreter creates our life story. Notably, evidence for the Interpreter has only been found in human beings (Gazzaniga 1998).

Relating the Interpreter to the human need for metaphysical explanation will draw together the psychological reasons for metaphysical dualism. I suggest a process whereby humans automatically (i.e. *nonreflectively*) see the world in terms of agents and other minds. Then, by dint of *reflection*, create a story that makes sense of the world in a human way, specifically, as an interaction of minds. It is the second step that is unique to humans.[14] The reason humans endow the world around them with human mental properties is that it is the manner in which humans *know* (i.e., it is epistemologically human, due to evolutionary considerations, to understand what is around them based on mental causes) and furthermore, doing so makes the world an understandable place. The fact that a species sees the world according to its own epistemological limitations is no surprise. What we must keep in mind though is that natural selection molds creatures that work, not creatures that know the true nature of reality.

In conclusion, research in experimental psychology supports the claim that humans are metaphysical dualists because we are intrinsically social animals with an innate, as well as reflective, penchant for making sense of the world in our common vocabulary, that of the mind. The deeply social nature of human beings will thread through the entire book, as we will see it provides the evolutionary basis for many of the seemingly high-level processes involved in consumer society, as well as providing one of the psychological foundations for *why we buy*.

Summary

This chapter offers a description of the first of the three fundamental characteristics of the *"default" model of the self*, the spiritual aspect: metaphysical dualism. Even though contemporary Americans are surrounded by technology (and thus metaphysical materialism), there are historical, religious, cultural and psychological reasons why metaphysical dualism remains our belief concerning the nature of reality. The inner self, or soul, implied in metaphysical dualism suggests that the individual is fundamental. We turn now to the consequences of this belief in the political characteristic of the *"default" model of the self* and *why we buy* in contemporary America: individualism.

Notes

1 Henceforth, dualism will be referred to as metaphysical dualism so as to avoid confusion with alternate meanings of the term "dualism" used in other fields.

2 These processes have been studied extensively by psychologists; for example, see the work of my mentor, Stanley B. Klein (2002).

3 For more on the historical and philosophical relation between the terms 'mind' and 'soul', see R. Gabriel (2009) *The Mind and the Soul*, video and paper accessible at www.mindscienceculture.com.

4 For Aquinas, the soul has individuality via its existence and actualization but in humans it is dual in that it is composed of primary matter (i.e. the physical body) and substantial form (i.e. the nonphysical soul); he breaks the latter further into intellect and will. Aquinas, among other accomplishments, laid the foundations for the Catholic Church to apply rational arguments to dogma.

5 *Res extensa* is substance that takes up space, in other words, is physical; *res cogitans* is substance that is mental and non-spatial, in other words, is nonphysical.

6 For one of many biting criticisms of metaphysical dualism and particularly Descartes' solution to the problem of the interaction between mind and body, see the first chapter of the philosophical classic: Ryle, G. (1949). *The Concept of Mind*. Chicago, IL: University of Chicago Press.

7 See Chapter Three for more on Romanticism's effect on the concept of self.

8 The consequences of this shift in understanding identity in America will be explored in Chapter Two on the essentialized individual and Chapter Three on interiorized expressivism.

9 See, among others, Ryle (1949), Dennett (1991).

10 In contemporary psychology, the term "innate" means born with genetic codes to create certain mind processes at specified developmental stages, not born with mind processes. For example, humans innately possess depth perception even though infants cannot see depth as soon as they are born.

11 With the exception of developmental disorders in the Autism spectrum (see the work of S. Baron-Cohen, 1995).

12 Nonhuman social animals seem to possess the first type of metaphysical dualism, insofar as they live in social groups, which require communication and expectation of behavior through belief and desire reasoning (McComb, Baker & Moss, 2005; Moss, 1988). Yet they do not seem to possess metaphysical dualism in its more intricate sense of postulating metaphysical entities to explain and guide life since it is not known to what extent nonhuman

animals engage in reflection. This field of animal meta-cognition is quite extensive; see for example the work of J. David Smith and colleagues (1998).

13 Michael Gazzaniga and his collaborators discovered this phenomenon of confabulation in the Left Hemisphere in people who had their hemispheres disconnected to halt debilitating epileptic seizures, referred to as Split Brain patients, see M. Gazzaniga (1998) *The Mind's Past*. University of California Press.

14 Many psychologists hold that reflective abilities are mediated by structures in the frontal lobe, specifically the prefrontal cortex that is significantly smaller in nonhuman animals (Damasio, 2011).

Chapter 2

Individualism: The Liberal Dream of the Rugged Individualist

This chapter introduces the political characteristic of the *"default" model of the self* in the context of American society: individualism. Individualism describes the institutional and professional dimension of the self and is apparent in our aspirations and how individuals relate to other individuals, that is, our social orientation. Although to some extent at the biological level we are each separate organisms, cultural circumstances, within society have an influence upon social orientation and the motives of our long- and short-term behaviors. In contemporary American culture, individualism is a strong cultural and historical determinant of our social orientation and the goals that motivate our actions since it structures how individuals understand their positions and aspirations in regard to others within society.[1] What follows is a description of individualism, as well as a its connection to how, where, and why the political and economic ideology of Liberalism originated and became dominant in America. The chapter closes with a description of a contrasting approach to structuring society that emerged as a critique of individualism. The purpose of this chapter is to provide a historical context of the individualist tradition that comprises the political dimension of the self and *why we buy* in contemporary American consumer society. Accordingly, a majority of what follows is a recounting of the seminal roots of individualism. The chapter concludes with a description of what I take to be a better framework for understanding the political dimension of the self, namely, its social context.

I. The Many Faces of Individualism

The meanings of the concept of individualism are best demarcated along national boundaries.[2] The German sense of individualism signifies self-fulfillment and the organic unity of the individual and society, whereas the French sense of the word was negative, referring to isolation and social dissolution due to an imbalance between self-interest and social solidarity. In America, the term became deeply connected to the economic system (capitalism) and Liberal democracy; it implied natural rights, a belief in free enterprise, and the American Dream (or, the "bootstrap" myth: that individuals sink or swim according solely to the merit of their work).[3] To be more precise, individualism is a superordinate concept that can be broken down into:

a) *The dignity of man*, that is, the intrinsic value of the individual human being;
b) *Autonomy*: "an individual's thought and action is his own and not determined by agencies or causes outside his control … (they are) autonomous to the degree to which he subjects

the pressures and norms with which he is confronted to conscious and critical evaluation, and forms intentions and reaches practical decisions as the result of independent and rational reflection" (Lukes, 1973, p. 52);

c) *Privacy*: an area in which the individual is or should be left alone by others and is able to do and think whatever he chooses; to pursue his own good in his own way,

d) *Self-development*: self-cultivation with a stress on qualitative uniqueness and individuality.[4]

Individualism includes the following doctrines:

a) *Abstract individualism*: individuals are considered abstractly as the primary unit of analysis. Individuals are considered as having interests, wants, purposes, needs, etc., while society and the State are portrayed as secondary sets of actual or possible social arrangements that respond more or less adequately to the requirements of individuals.

b) *Political Individualism*: individuals are independent rational beings who are the sole generators of their own wants and preferences and are the best judges of their own interests. In the modern era, the notion of free elections represents the height of political individualism.

c) *Economic Individualism*: individuals require a system of free trade, competition, and private property, rather than planning, bureaucratization, welfare, and redistributive policies of government. According to this doctrine, a free-market economy is the natural economic infrastructure.[5]

The four elements of individualism—dignity, autonomy, privacy, and self-development—are essential elements in our notions of equality and liberty. Human dignity, or respect for other people, lies at the heart of equality, while autonomy, privacy, and self-development constitute our notions of liberty and freedom. Through this analysis we see that the four elements that constitute individualism are intimately related, both logically and conceptually. Conceptually, these characteristics of individualism combine to form a central animating political concept in America: Liberalism, the combination of equality, liberty, and freedom of thought. Louis Hartz's (1955) notion of a Liberal, or American democrat, is a person who believes in individual liberty, equality, and capitalism and who regards the human marketplace, where a person succeeds or fails by his or her own efforts and ability, as the proper testing ground of achievement; basically, a combination of political and economic individualism. What is presupposed in this definition is abstract individualism, the assumption that the individual is the main unit of analysis, that we must start with the individual and only later arrive at the community. These cultural determinants of social orientation, namely, the desire for equality, liberty, and freedom embedded in political, economic, and abstract individualism, encapsulate the institutional and professional dimension of the *"default" model of the self*. Let us now turn to individualism's distinct tradition in American political thought.

II. The Origins of Liberalism in America

The basis for the American Liberal-Democratic state is to be found in the political theory and governance of England in the seventeenth century, the essential ingredient of which was a new belief in the value and the rights of the individual (MacPherson, 1962). This section provides a partial survey of the historical origins of certain political strands embedded within contemporary America's notion of the good society.

The political philosopher Thomas Hobbes (1588–1679) in his *Leviathan* (1651, 2000) argues that men are machines moved to and fro by two basic motions—the desire for power and the fear of death. The desire for power leads to "the state of nature" where life is solitary, poor, nasty, brutish, and short, whereas "civil society" arises from the fear of death, as well as the desire for success in obtaining the things one desires. Hobbes argues that we must each read ourselves (i.e., self-reflect), for it is through this activity we discover all men are the same. Whatever moral obligations follow for one will follow for all, whatever desire one sees in oneself will also be present in other men. According to the American political scientist C. B. MacPherson (1962), individualism originated in Hobbes's highly individualist postulates: Hobbes deduced political rights and obligations from the interest and will of an abstract notion of the individual, while furthermore emphasizing the equal moral worth of every human being. Hobbes's legacy in America, which I describe more fully in the next section, is *abstract individualism*, the notion of the individual as the starting point for any analysis of social structures.

The next influential thinker in the Liberal tradition is the British philosopher John Locke (1632–1704), and in particular his "Second Treatise of Government" (1690, 1980). Locke defines civil freedom as having a legislated standing rule to live by common to all members of society. This standing rule is the liberty to follow one's own will in all things and not be at the mercy of the arbitrary will of other men. Locke's crucial conceptual advance is the idea of property: whatsoever one removes out of the state of nature and mixes with one's labor, joining to it something that is his own, is thereby his property.[6] In conjunction with this idea, the purpose of civil government for Locke is the protection of property. Locke's ideas continued Hobbes's methodological individualism while also cementing property to the individual such that within a Liberal society being an individual became constitutively tied to owning property. Locke's legacy for Liberalism in contemporary American society is the importance of property in defining its citizens, and the notion of social equality such that each citizen ought to be free from coercion.[7]

But Liberalism is more than just a theory about property and freedom from coercion; it is also crucially invested in the notion of liberty, or freedom of thought. The major thinker in this tradition is the British philosopher John Stuart Mill (1806–1873), who puts forth the claim that,

> The appropriate region of human liberty comprises the inward domain of consciousness: demanding liberty of conscience in the most comprehensive sense, liberty of thought and feeling, absolute freedom of opinion and sentiment of all subjects practical and

speculative. Liberty of tastes and pursuits; of framing the plan of our life to suit our own character; of doing as we like, subject to such consequences as may follow without impediment from our fellow creatures, so long as what we do does not harm them even though they should think our conduct foolish.

(Mill, 1859, 2002, p. 15)

This quote exemplifies Mill's endorsement of individuality: the combination of autonomy and self-development, or more simply, uniqueness. Mill claims that individuality diversifies, animates, and elevates life; indeed, genius, Mill claims, springs from individuality and originality. In this way, social progress depends upon the amount of individuality present in a given society. Thus, the greatest obstacles to social progress are custom and tradition that stifle individuality. Mill developed upon the concept of Liberalism and influenced contemporary American society through his notions of liberty of choice and freedom of thought. He also extolled individuality as essential to social progress.[8]

From these three British thinkers—Thomas Hobbes, John Locke, and John Stuart Mill—came the major historical foundations of American Liberalism and individualism, specifically, the value of liberty, equality, property, freedom of thought and action, and individuality.

III. The Rise of Liberalism in America

How did Liberalism become such an important cultural determinant of social orientation in America? The answer to this question involves the following themes: American exceptionalism in the New World, democracy (i.e., a system of government where all citizens are represented in governing bodies and are equal before the law), and the notion of a "class-less" society.[9] When discussing the unique history of America's Liberal individualist tradition, we must keep in mind French political thinker and historian Alexis de Tocqueville's (1835) famous adage: "[T]he great advantage of the Americans is, that they have arrived at a state of democracy without having to endure a democratic revolution; and that they are born equal, instead of becoming so" (*Democracy in America*, book 2, chapter 3).

The unique political theory legacy of America is that it began with John Locke and stayed with him; Locke dominates American political thought as no thinker anywhere dominates the political thought of a nation, he is a massive national cliché (Hartz, 1955).[10] There are a number of characteristics that differentiate America from its direct European heritage, most notably, America did not have a feudal period, strictly speaking, and lacks a strong institutional tradition of reactionism, like formal socialism.[11] In many ways, the American Revolution was a de facto separation from the complicated and troubled Old World. According to American political scientist Louis Hartz (1955), the New World does not comprehend sovereign power; it has an altered sense of the past, which excludes Old-World bourgeois class passion. Hartz emphasizes America's vast and "almost charming" innocence.

There was also a change in the social fabric of the New World that was crucial to the development of Liberalism in America: "[T]he process of expanding the European category of the petit bourgeois shattered it and created a new hybrid citizen who was a laborer and an entrepreneur ... a peasant and a capitalist farmer" (Hartz, 1955, p. 91). This new type of bourgeois fulfilled Locke's vision of an independent individual citizen defined by his property. What we see in the New World is a restructuring of social hierarchy and orientation from sovereign rule to democracy, where individual voters are represented in civil government by their votes. This form of *political individualism* has vast consequences for the social orientation of citizens (Schudson, 1998). According to American political and social historian Robert Wiebe (1992), what democracy ultimately supplies us with is a way of conducting our common affairs. But democracy is more than self-governance, it also includes something culturally specific, in America this element is individual self-determination; citizens rule collectively, as well as individually (Wiebe, 1992). Those in power had the authority to rule collectively, while gainful employment gave individuals economic freedom, such that from the political system of democracy came both community self-governance and economic self-determination, or economic individualism (Wiebe, 1992). Robert Wiebe goes on to link this tendency to self-rule and economic individualism with the social and cultural changes of the late eighteenth century. At the same time that majority consensus became a prominent political entity in Europe, the individual became the heart of American democracy. This was initially achieved by expanding autonomy in the guise of choices available to individuals in terms of consumer markets, occupations, and lifestyles. Choices also became encapsulated in the Bill of Rights (1791). Americans understood rights as belonging to individuals apart from their communities; this was a significant development in abstract individualism.

Essentially, democracy in America institutionalized political, abstract, and economic individualism. Furthermore, Mill's concept of individuality held great importance in American democracy vis-à-vis emergent class relations in the New World. In many ways, the myth of pulling oneself up by their bootstraps became the representative model for how class functioned in the New World. The success of this model partly depends upon the value of self-determination within an individualist society and is intrinsically tied to Locke's linking of citizenship to property and hopes for granting social equality to all. In the "bootstrap" myth, a given individual's economic situation is determined by his economic individualism. In this element of American exceptionalism we see evidence of two underlying claims: that status is simply merit-based and that freedom from the binding structures of tradition, caste, and rule under the Noble class lead to a unique form of economic freedom and a range of otherwise unreachable economic and political possibilities.

In summary, democracy institutionalized abstract, political, and economic individualism, while the myth of a "classless society" claimed that any citizen could pick himself up by his bootstraps. This was in direct contrast to Old World social structures and enshrined abstract individualism as the main determinant of social orientation through the values of liberty, equality, property, freedom of thought and action, and individuality. It was these institutions that legitimated and cemented Liberal individualism in the American political arena.

Individualism in Contemporary American Society

In practical terms, what does individualism—the addition of Hobbesian, Lockean, and Millsian political theory—amount to in contemporary America? C. B. Macpherson (1962) claims America's Liberal political heritage resulted in possessive individualism, freedom from dependence on others that ensures one only enters into relations that are voluntary, and since an individual owns his own abilities—for which he owes society nothing, it might be added—an individual is free to alienate his abilities to the market. Furthermore, each individual's freedom can rightfully be limited by the obligations necessary to secure the same freedom for others because political society is simply a Lockean contrivance for the protection of an individual's property and the maintenance of relations of property between proprietors. MacPherson highlights the following sociocultural changes that fueled possessive individualism: what had been a unified individual became a play of many characters in that the multiplication of settings created a need for different values depending upon the context, the most basic division of settings was the separation between work and privacy, or leisure; and, due to the importance of self-development, the public persona became little more than a façade for a burgeoning private life that flourished through exploration and self-development.[12]

What became the driving force of individualism in contemporary America was a vision of universalized rights; rights tied to the urge for individual fulfillment, self-development, and liberty. Having economic individualism as the crucial locus in the notion of rights shifted the function of representative bodies (e.g., the federal government) because rights began to be considered as only serving to reinforce individual fulfillment, which simultaneously led to the decay of shared social needs.[13] Possessive individualism represents a culmination of individualism in contemporary America and a social orientation that focuses on the individual rather than the society. For MacPherson (1962), the dilemma of contemporary Liberal democracy is that it must continue with the assumptions of possessive individualism even though this social orientation is insufficient for structuring social obligation appropriately, because society depends upon a notion of the public good that is not necessarily included in the social orientation of individualism.

With this critique in hand it becomes apparent that Liberal individualism has been described so far but nothing has been said about other social orientations that are also part of America's history. In the last 40 years, for example, in direct contestation of abstract individualism, there has been a sustained critique of Liberal and Neoliberal traditions, that emphasizes the centrality of community and social relations over the omnipotence of the individual. A description of this critique of Liberalism will provide us with a fuller understanding of the limits of individualism in the broader context of American political thought and provide us with the model of an alternative social orientation. This social context also connects us to claims about the social nature of human beings made in Chapter 1. The model described in the next section will factor in the concluding chapter on the future of consumer society in America.

IV. Communitarianism

Although individualism is the dominant model of social orientation in the institutional and professional dimension of the self in contemporary America, I find communitarianism to be a more accurate portrayal of how the self is embedded and defined by its social context. Furthermore, I claim it ought to provide a more secure model for an appropriate social orientation. The main critique of individualism by the communitarians is that social attachments determine the nature of the self, and thus individuals are defined by the community of which they comprise a nonvoluntary part, in this way the abstract individualist image of an autonomous self is false; the self is actually intrinsically comprised of its social relations and cannot stand alone. According to sociologist Amitai Etzioni (1998), communitarians believe in the freedom of individuals but also in a public good in the form of the importance of shared governance structures that pool our interests and efforts toward satisfying social needs. Etzioni defines community as a web of social relations that encompass shared meaning and shared values. Within communitarianism, there is an emphasis both on the significance of social forces, community, and social bonds, as well as a balance between social forces and the person, community and autonomy, the common good and liberty—in short, a blend of individual rights and social responsibilities. Communitarianism is a double-pronged critique of Liberal Individualism: firstly, it is a methodological critique stating that abstract individualism is false in that the only way to understand human behavior is to refer to individuals in their social, cultural, and historical contexts. Secondly, it is a normative critique in that Liberal individualism gives rise to morally unsatisfactory consequences, for example, the impossibility of achieving genuine community, the unjust distribution of goods, and the neglect of ideas of the good life that do not center around the individual and property (Avineri & de-Shalit, 1992).

Whereas liberty in the Early Republic (1789–1823) was understood as a function of democratic institutions and dispersed power, liberty in contemporary America is defined as an individual's guarantee against instances when the will of the majority may curtail their freedom of thought and action. In this scheme, rights serve as trumps. The communitarians claim that politics have been displaced from smaller forms of association and relocated to a far more general form, that is, power has shifted away from democratic institutions toward institutions that are actually insulated from democratic pressures. As the scale of social and political organization has become more comprehensive, the terms of our collective identity have become more fragmented and the forms of political life have outrun the common purpose needed to sustain them (Sandel, 1992). The weakening of democracy's community component strengthened the individual component such that expression from the citizens disappeared from political life and only surfaces in our private personal lives (Wiebe, 1992).[14]

Canadian philosopher Charles Taylor's (1992) critical description of individualism emphasizes how the doctrines of social contract theory, which arose in the seventeenth century with Hobbes and Locke, created a vision of society constituted by individuals for the fulfillment of primarily individual ends. This possessive individualism defends the priority of the individual and his rights over society, and in many cases presents society as simply a guarantor of property. Such abstract individualist theories that emphasize the primacy of individual rights,

> accept a principle ascribing rights to men as binding unconditionally on men as such but they do not accept as similarly unconditional a principle of belonging or obligation, these are seen as derivative through our consent or through its being to our advantage.
>
> (Taylor, 1992, p. 188)

Taylor claims American citizens find it reasonable to start a political theory with an assertion of individual rights because of atomism, a theory that affirms the self-sufficiency of man alone. Yet, there is a crucial flaw in this atomistic framework: asserting a right has an essential conceptual background, the primacy of rights is not independent from considerations of human nature and social conditions—if these capacities can only rise in a certain kind of society then this is proof that we ought to belong or sustain this kind of society so that we may even have the possibility of individual rights. Therefore, atomism, the basis of the individualist framework of rights and an individualist social orientation depends on the greater context of a society that allows such rights to exist and be perpetuated. This line of thinking poses a limit to the individualist idea of society.

Liberals have responded to these communitarian critiques by emphasizing the malleability of Liberalism. For example, American political scientist Richard Flathman (1998) posits individuality and self-development as the highest ideals of Liberalism, ideals whose pursuit requires an abundant social and political plurality in addition to the widest possible freedom of action. Flathman's willful Liberalism is a way of centering the onus of the continuance of Liberalism and democracy on each individual's will and on the irreducible diversity of goods, ends, and ideals (Flathman, 1998). It is a world of free individuals who are constantly in contact with the wills of other free individuals, it is concerned less with "ends and purposes, rights and duties, and more with the manner in which each individual does whatever she chooses to do" (Flathman, 1998, p. 7). The primary political virtue in willful Liberalism is civility, a virtue tied to the dignity of man and dependent upon a broader social orientation. Flathman's response cleverly highlights the importance of social interaction within liberalism as a contrast to abstract individualism, but his theory ultimately fails to sufficiently address the rigid limits of political and economic individualism.

In conclusion, communitarianism is not part of the *"default" model of the self* but it does offer an important alternative social orientation through delineating the limits of the current dominant political characteristic of the self, individualism. Communitarianism may offer a way forward for conceptualizing citizenship in contemporary American democracy.

Summary

This chapter provided a description of the political characteristic of the *"default" model of the self* and *why we buy* in the context of the core structural frameworks and institutions in contemporary American society. Abstract, political, and economic individualism, their roots in British political theory, their practical consequences in Liberalism, and their development into and within the democratic state were all discussed. The chapter closed with the introduction of communitarianism as a limit to the individualist model of social orientation. Metaphysical dualism and individualism together imply an independent interior space; a description of this space as it relates to *why we buy* is provided in Chapter 3.

Notes

1 Chapters 5 and 6 include descriptions of the social and cultural determinants of social orientation in other cultures.
2 Political and social theorist Steven Lukes's (1973) excellent, and concise, book on the subject serves as the source of my description of the historical and conceptual background of Individualism.
3 Furthermore, the American Dream refers to the specific case of when an individual is an economic success in terms of the standard accoutrements of the bourgeois class.
4 See Chapter 3 for more on this notion in the context of the Romantic Movement.
5 Lukes (1973) also includes:

Religious Individualism: an individual believer does not need intermediaries; he has primary responsibility for his own spiritual destiny and has the right and duty to have his own relationship with his own god in his own way and by his own effort.
Ethical Individualism: morality is essentially an individual choice, this is usually paired with ethical egoism, that is, the sole moral object of individual's actions is his own benefit.
Epistemological Individualism: a philosophical doctrine about the nature of knowledge that states the source of knowledge lies within the individual (e.g., Descartes' *I think therefore I am* as discussed in Chapter 1), and,
Methodological Individualism: a doctrine asserting that all attempts to explain social phenomena are to be rejected unless they are couched wholly in terms of facts about individuals.

6   It being by him removed from the common state nature has placed it in, it has by this labor something annexed to it that excludes the common right of other men. For this labor being the unquestionable property of the laborer, no man but he can have a right to what he has added his labor to.

(Locke, 2004, ch. 5, section 27)

7   Freedom is not a liberty for every one to do what he lists and not to be tied by any laws; but freedom of men under government is to have a standing rule to live by, common to every one of that society and made by the legislative power erected in it, a liberty to follow my own will in all things where the rule prescribes not, and not to be subject to the inconstant, uncertain, unknown, arbitrary will of another man.

(Locke, 2004, p. 14)

8   This emphasis on individuality is also an important cultural determinant of the personal expressivist characteristic of the *"default" model of the self* described in Chapter 3.
9   See the conclusion for an analysis of class and the deeper relation between democracy and individualism.
10 When Locke came to new world, his theory became a description of fact: the theoretical social norms of Europe were inverted into the factual premises of America (Hartz, 1955).
11 This interpretation is not without controversy, for example, see Haskell, T. L. (2000). "Taking exception to exceptionalism." *Reviews in American History*, Vol. 28, No. 1 (March), pp. 151–166.
12 This element of the *"default" model of the self* shall be discussed in detail in Chapter 3.
13 See Lizbeth Cohen's (2003) *A consumer's republic*, and George Lipsitz (1998) *Consumer spending as state project: Yesterday's solutions and today's problems*, for excellent documentation of this shift in the early twentieth century.
14 The theme of expression is taken up in Chapter 3, and the efficacy of government in response to citizens is revisited in the conclusion.

Chapter 3

Expressivism: I Sing Myself

This chapter provides a description of the personal characteristic of the *"default" model of the self* in America, the dimension that encapsulates our notion of mental well-being and serves as an important source of our desires and hopes. Expressivism is the belief that every person holds inside him a deep reservoir of feelings, thoughts, and impulses, and that these deep processes can and should be expressed.[1] This model of the mind seems so obvious that it is hard to imagine that people did not always think of their minds (and selves) as containing an inner space. Canadian philosopher Charles Taylor who coined the term expressivism in *Sources of the Self* (1989) locates this cultural shift in our model of the mind, and the self, when the concept of the inner voice gained great importance historically after philosopher and author Jean-Jacques Rousseau's *Confessions* (1782): one of the first autobiographies to focus on deep emotional sentiments and the natural innocence of man in nature. He summarizes it well in the following passage:

> We can now know from within us, from the impulses of our own being, what Nature marks as significant, and our ultimate happiness is to live in conformity with this voice, that is, to be entirely ourselves.
>
> (Taylor, 1989, p. 362)

Embedded in expressivism is the further belief that if we access Nature (i.e., that which is true and authentic) through our inner voice and impulses, then our main access to being *real* or true to ourselves is through the expression, or articulation, of our interior space. In *Habits of the Heart* (1996), sociologists Robert Bellah et al. describe the contemporary importance of expressivism in our personal (i.e., private/domestic) lives; they describe how personal life developed into a space of liberation and fulfillment as contrasted with our workplace/public lives, which they characterize as utilitarian. Ultimately, expressivism promotes an ethics of individualism and individuality as well as the concept of metaphysical dualism in that it conceptualizes a separate inner dimension of the mind to which each individual has sole access. Expressivism thus serves as a convenient finale of this first part of the book as it completes my description of the *"default" model of the self* and *why we buy* by drawing together individualism and metaphysical dualism in the personal/practical dimension of the self.

My contention in this chapter is that expressivism, best exemplified in the figure of the artist who reveals himself authentically through his craft, influenced society in a transformative manner that is apparent in the beliefs and desires of individuals in contemporary America. What follows is a description of the historical and cultural roots of the expressivist strand of the *"default" model of the self* through the accounts of the inward turn of Protestantism and Romanticism, the post-Freudian psychological man, and the concept of authenticity. This chapter—and the first part of the book—closes with an explanation of the central concept that bridges the *"default" model of the self* and consumer society: *taste*.

I. Inward Turn

The first theme to be introduced in characterizing expressivism is the inward turn: a shift of emphasis from the outer world to the inner world. There are both religious and cultural-historical roots of this element of the contemporary notion of the self in America. The philosopher Michel Foucault (1993) traced the inward turn to the dogmatic notion in Christianity that to have a self is to purge its contents into the world. Christianity dictates that one must sacrifice the self in verbalization toward the dramatic end of being true to themselves and true to God by divulging hidden desires. Such a process entails a constant interpretation of the inner voice of the self. This crucial element in Christianity, what Foucault dubs the confessional self, helped to create and perpetuate the idea that one's self is a deep reservoir of thoughts, feelings, and desires. For Foucault, confession makes us amenable to social control and furthermore, makes us dependent upon confession for the maintenance and perpetuation of an inner voice. Foucault calls these procedures the technology of the self, by which he means operations people undertake on their own bodies, souls, thoughts, and motives. For Foucault these are ultimately techniques of domination and agency since confession in this framework serves as a form of monitoring, through comparing one's inner thought to the truth and authenticity of the purity of the soul in the eyes of God. Verbalization of our inner desires in confession must be a permanent interpretive activity that goes as deep as possible into one's thoughts toward converting hidden evils into visible goodness. Ultimately, we have to sacrifice the privacy of the self to discover the truth about it. Foucault concludes by pondering whether the self is nothing but the history of the technologies we have employed to empty our innermost thoughts into the world. This question strikes at the heart of another debate that took place in the seventeenth and eighteenth centuries concerning the question of whether the inner space of the self always existed, or was actually created by the practice of confession. Regardless of the answer to this complicated question, which requires interpretation of various historical records, it is clear that the last three hundred years have seen a wider appreciation of the concept of an inner voice, much of this expansion is due to the cultural movement of Romanticism to which we now turn.

Romanticism

Romanticism, an artistic movement that took place between approximately 1770 and 1830, was characterized by an emphasis on individuality, an interest in innate, intuitive, and instinctive behaviors, great value placed upon self-development, and an understanding of the self in terms of psychological depth. Philosopher and historian of ideas Isaiah Berlin (2001) recounts how the main theorist of the movement, philosopher Friedrich W. J. Schelling (1775–1854), claimed that man is the conscious part of nature and therefore the function of man as artist is to delve into his own inner space and, through violent internal struggle, bring it to consciousness. This artistic process is apparent in the British arch-Romantic poet William Wordsworth's (1770–1850) claim that the poet's task is to reveal the depths of the human soul. The Romantic Movement was an attempt to impose an aesthetic model upon reality and went so far as to claim that all aspects of life should obey the rules of art. According to Berlin, this inward turn occurred because the natural road toward human fulfillment was blocked and so a natural human response that followed was to lock oneself up in an inner citadel away from the evils of the world. He claims that this was the mood of a large proportion of the Romantics in Germany, specifically a branch of Protestantism called the German Pietists. This sentiment resulted in an intense inner life and a great deal of very moving, highly personal, and violently emotional literature. It also brought along a disdain for the intellect and a violent hatred of the snobbery and urbanity evident in the European cultural capital of Paris.[2] A central thinker in this German incarnation of the Romantic movement, the philosopher Johann Gottfried von Herder (1744–1803), posited the following popular and revolutionary idea: one of the fundamental functions of human beings is to express, and therefore whatever a man does expresses his full nature. Furthermore, he claimed a work of art is the voice of one man addressing himself to other men; it is the expression of its maker's attitude to life. Art in this context is a form of communication. Herder's views on art have led to our contemporary formulation of the creative process as a direct link to Nature and Truth that each person holds within. Furthermore, it is one's duty to mine this inner space toward artistic expression, which is a positive act of catharsis (i.e., an explosion of unconscious ideas and emotional energy from an interior hidden space to an exterior visible space).[3] Romanticism served as the ideology of a burgeoning artist class within which the increasingly respected practice of art came to be understood as the revelation of an inner space; this is a crucial element in the history of expressivism (Campbell, 1987). As we shall see in Chapter 4, Romanticism remains an influential strand in contemporary society in the form of the counterculture.

II. Psychological Man

Another important cultural moment in the creation of the expressivist characteristic of the *"default" model of the self* is Psychoanalysis. American sociologist and cultural critic Phillip Rieff in *The Mind of the Moralist* (1959) argues that the legacy of Sigmund Freud is a new conception of mankind he calls psychological man.[4] Psychological man is the child of technology (both Foucauldian and scientific), he is not committed to public life, is antiheroic, counts his satisfactions and dissatisfactions through a careful economy of the inner life, and lives by the ideal of insight into mastery of his own personality. Salvation for the psychological man can only come through contemplation and manipulation of inner space. This modern creature is the child of Protestantism, the Enlightenment, and democracy; he takes on the attitude of scientist with himself alone as the ultimate object of his science, the improvement of the self through an economy of the inner space is his main concern (Rieff, 1968).

This model of psychological man stems from psychologist Sigmund Freud's conceptualization of the nature of the mind, starting with the claim that our inner nature lies hidden in the Unconscious (Freud, 1916). The truth is hidden from even oneself, just like in the confessional self of Christianity where sins are hidden. The solution to the self not knowing what is going on in the depths of the mind is psychoanalytic therapy. The aim of therapy is the ego's exploration, or confession, of itself, with an emphasis on deciphering deep interior spaces, like dreams. In Freud's conceptualization of the mind, man is pictured as an aesthetic animal for whom the creation of art provides the occasion to contemplate one's inner space in a frozen gesture that ultimately unburdens the self of its hidden truths. The process whereby a piece of the unconscious becomes manifested in a way that is not explicitly a part of one's neurosis is called sublimation. Art is the paradigmatic example of sublimation for Freud, since it functions as a safety valve by expressing unconscious struggles in a manner that is not detrimental to the self (Freud, 1916). Psychoanalysis is a tutorial in the managerial virtues of prudence and compromise, it teaches one how to stop censorship so that the inner space can come through. The psychoanalyst can be likened to an investment broker of emotions, a secular spiritual guide. The product of Psychoanalysis as a post-religious ethic is psychological man who becomes his own religion—a religion in which taking care of oneself is the ritual and health is the ultimate dogma. After Freud, individualism took "a great and perhaps final step towards that mature calm feeling which comes from having nothing to hide …" (Rieff, 1968, p. 60). Psychoanalysis was initially devised by Freud to protect the public life against further encroachments or deviancy within the inner life. For Freud, neurosis is a range of conditions wherein a person is unable to function in society because of the deep emotional trauma to the inner space that become manifest in inappropriate behaviors. In modern times, "when so little can be taken for granted, and when the meaningfulness of social existence no longer grants an inner life at peace with itself, every man must become something of a genius about himself," such that we now have a culture made up mainly of virtuosi of the self (Rieff, 1968, p. 32). Psychoanalysis focuses on the aesthetic problem of expression, with the assumption that if we were all artists there would be no neurosis because health is a function of the appropriate expression of the inner voice. Rieff claims that in contemporary times scientists fulfill a position formerly held by the clergy, the role of spiritual preceptor, while the modern artist is responsible for representing what humans are trying to become in an effort to escape the pressures of our traumatized and claustrophobic inner spaces. The work of art in this sense is cathartic and therapeutic, it is an emotional practice with the aim of destroying the tension between inner and outer life (Rieff, 1968).

What is revolutionary in modern culture is the shift from a model of trying to control and renounce one's impulses and needs to a model of impulse release, wherein one is controlled by an infinite variety of wants, raised to the status of needs, that attempt to achieve new ways of fulfilling the impulse release (Rieff, 1968). The self of psychological man only finds salvation in breaking communal identities and in suspicion of all normative institutions; this new anti-culture aims at an eternal interim ethic of release from inherited controls, an abstract individualism. This has repercussions in the direction of individualism for one's social orientation:

> by psychologizing about themselves endlessly, modern men are learning to use internality against the primacy of any particular organization of personality. If this restructuring succeeds, then human autonomy from compulsions of culture may follow the freedoms already won from the compulsions of nature. It is conceivable that distinctions between inner and outer, private and public life will become trivial; all can be exploited for individual's well-being.

> (Rieff, 1968, p. 21)

Psychoanalysis is a secular individualist ethic tied to the confessional self of Christianity and the therapeutic need to focus on the inner space. These forms of expressivism, which conceive of the self as a reservoir and depict self-exploration and therapy as life goals of the utmost importance, are most clearly observed in the self-actualization and human potential movements of the 1960s and 1970s in America, for example, in Primal Scream Therapy and the work of psychologist R. D. Laing.[5] This emphasis on the importance of the inner life has its critics, dubbed the New Narcissists, who consider the need to express to be detrimental to moral and community values.[6] Rieff (1968) has his own pessimistic conclusion declaring that,

> a sense of well-being has become the end, rather than a by-product of striving after some superior communal end.

> (Rieff, 1968, p. 261)

Claims of narcissism notwithstanding, psychological man, the confessional self, and the Romantic Movement are elements of the expressivism that have consequences for who we think we are and the orientation of our personal goals. We shall take this analysis deeper by asking the following questions: what is the ideal exploration of the inner space? And what signals a successful expression of the self?

III. Authenticity

A central aspect of expressivism is the positive value given to achievement of a true, or accurate translation between inner space and its expression: authenticity. In *Sincerity and Authenticity* (1972), American literary critic Lionel Trilling claims that sincerity—the expression of the self underneath its public roles—is a late addition to European culture. Trilling gives a historical analysis of this phenomenon, best quoted in full:

at a certain point in history men became individuals, before that man did not have an awareness of internal space, he did not imagine himself in more than one role … it is when he becomes an individual that a man lives more and more in private rooms (and) begins to use the word "self" not as a mere reflexive but as an autonomous noun referring to that in a person which is really and intrinsically he, as that which he must cherish for its own sake and show to the world for the sake of good faith. Authenticity is a more strenuous moral experience than sincerity, it serves as a more exigent conception of the self and of what being true to it consists in, it casts a wider reference to the universe and man's place in it, paired with a less acceptant and genial view of the social circumstances of life. Authenticity took over from sincerity and stood for downward movement through all cultural superstructures to some place wither all movement ends and begins.

(Trilling, 1972, p. 24)

The nineteenth-century British poet and sage Matthew Arnold gives a clear and beautiful description of this phenomenon in practice:

Below the surface-stream, shallow and light,
of what we say we feel—below the stream,
as light, of what we think we feel—there flows
with noiseless current strong, obscure and deep,
the central stream of what we feel indeed.[7]

The most important thinkers in this lineage of authenticity are Jean-Jacques Rousseau and Sigmund Freud. In his *Confessions* (1782), Rousseau claimed the purpose of an authentic life is to create and present to others a portrait that was true to Nature in every way. Furthermore, he claims man lives in a new context of industrial society in which the public and the body are obstacles between the authentic self and its authentic expression. This is similar to Freud's psychological man who must bare the inner depths of his unconscious mind authentically to alleviate neurosis and the Romantic who battles to display the inner self in a work of art. Psychoanalysis is a secular technology of the self because, in addition to being a continuous confession, there is an additional stage of a scientific truth to the matter: whether the confession was successful at alleviating the mental disorder, that is, whether or not the confession was authentic. Authenticity in these models serves as the ideal of exploration of the self insofar as it constitutes mental well-being.

The roots of the concept of the Unconscious and subsequently authentic inner space are in a systematic search for an underlying truth, they offer a theory of unmasking. This approach was used by the seventeenth-century French moralist La Rochefoucauld, nineteenth-century German philosophers Arthur Schopenhauer, Friedrich Nietzsche, and the economic philosopher Karl Marx, not to mention nineteenth-century Norwegian playwright Henrik Ibsen.[8] This approach accords with an entrenched belief that beneath the appearance of every human phenomenon, there lies concealed a discrepant actuality, and that intellectual, practical, and moral advantages are to be gained by forcibly bringing the deeper authentic self to light. Authenticity is the goal of this unmasking process and the authentic self is precisely the inner self, or soul, of metaphysical dualism described in Chapter 1. In the *"default" model of the self*, the personal/practical expression is authentic only insofar as it brings to light the metaphysical inner self.

In *The Ethics of Authenticity* (1991), the philosopher Charles Taylor gives a more complex story about the relation between the moral ideal of authenticity and the development of a culture of self-fulfillment described in the second part of this book as consumer society. Taylor claims that an ethic of authenticity was born at the end of the eighteenth century by building on earlier forms of individualism, namely, Descartes' metaphysical dualism as discussed in Chapter 1, John Locke's political individualism as discussed in Chapter 2, and Romanticism as discussed earlier in this chapter. For Taylor, the roots of the ethic of authenticity lie in the central notion of many religious and folk systems of belief, that humans are endowed with a moral sense. The notion of authenticity developed out of a displacement of the moral accent in this idea: rather than being in touch with the "right thing to do," we are in touch with our "true selves." Taylor claims that being in touch with one's inner self takes on independent and crucial moral significance, it becomes something we have to attain to be true and full human beings; in a secular culture, rather than being in touch with God, the only moral source we can draw from is the self within. This new importance placed on being true to oneself suggests that one misses the point of life and what it means to be human if one does not focus on being in touch with one's authentic inner self. In articulating one's originality one also defines one's self and realizes a potentiality that is one's own. This background of the ideal of authenticity and the goals of self-fulfillment and self-development gives moral force and positive value to the concept of authenticity and grounds the importance of being true to one's self (Taylor, 1991).

A connection is therefore evident between the ethic of authenticity and expressivism: authenticity is the search of the self for itself and in this process of seeking authenticity, the self is made, that is why creative acts can become the ultimate goal (Guignon, 2004). The concept of authenticity connects the themes thus far presented in this chapter as it explains the need, and positive value, given to connecting with an inner space through confession, art, or therapy. In addition, it connects expressivism to the belief in metaphysical dualism because authenticity relies upon the concept of an inner self, or soul, that underlies all other manifestations of the self.

IV. Taste

It is has come time to draw together the three characteristics of the *"default" model of the self* described in the first part of the book and turn toward the consequences of this model of the self for contemporary consumer society in America in the second part of the book. The inward turns of the confessional self, Romanticism, and psychological man have in contemporary American consumer society been turned outward as personal values, or sets of values, manifested in the notion of *taste*. In a post-Romantic and post-psychoanalytic society, the act of expression is no longer reserved for artistic creation; expression can now be achieved through what we decide to buy from among the huge set of possibilities. After Romanticism and Psychoanalysis, everyone is potentially an artist because everyone can mine their inner space to create or express their selves (Guignon, 2004). That is, what one decides to buy and how one organizes one's life, are manifestations of one's *taste* and are therefore acts of expression that reveal one's inner space, one's authentic self. In a consumer society, *taste* is the positive confession of the inner self of an individual. The conceptual background of the Romantic and psychoanalytic interpretation of art has given way to a parallel interpretation of the customization of lifestyles and the aesthetization of everyday consumption practices. The current technology of the self is choice since the choices revealed in one's lifestyle are a form of expression through self-fashioning and, when taken to extremes, self-fetishization.[9] *Taste* and style are expressivist manifestations of the individualist inner self. To consume the fancied need of a particular lifestyle is to manifest one's *taste* and therefore one's authentic identity. One of the psychological reasons *why we buy* is to reveal our inner selves to others.

But what determines the choices we make? French sociologist, anthropologist, and philosopher Pierre Bourdieu (1984) claims that *taste* is a symbolic social mechanism for organizing the distribution of resources. *Taste* itself depends upon habitus—a system of dispositions that organizes the individual's capacity to act. Habitus is evident in an individual's taken-for-granted preferences about the validity of his/her *taste*, it is itself shaped primarily in childhood by internalization of a particular set of material conditions, in this way habitus is linked to an individual's socioeconomic and cultural position. For Bourdieu, basic divides in *taste* are due to different class experiences in society. For example, according to British sociologist Colin Campbell (1987), aristocracy equates *taste* with conformity to carefully defined standards of propriety, whereas the middle classes regard *taste* as a sign of moral and spiritual worth. The main determinants of *taste* are age and class (the latter identified as socioeconomic level, i.e., income, occupation and education), this is because every cultural product requires a built-in educational requirement necessary for its appreciation (Gans, 1974). For American sociologist Herbert Gans, America is made up of a number of taste cultures that reveal people's values; these taste cultures differ in their expression of aesthetic standards and ability to put feelings into an aesthetic vocabulary. Both Bourdieu and Gans's explanations of the causes of *taste* lead to the conclusion that *taste* and the inner self it expresses are intrinsically shaped by social determinants.

Summary

This chapter provides a description of the inward turn through religion, psychology, and the positive value given to artistic expression. Furthermore, I developed the idea that the authentic inner space depends upon metaphysical dualism, and then connected expressivism to the concept of *taste*, bringing together the book's thesis that one of the psychological reasons behind *why we buy* is, the social need to reveal our inner selves to others through the creative act of choice. If we take *taste* to be a representation of the inner self and we take *taste* to be determined by social conditions, then the self is a natural phenomenon shaped by its social, economic, and historical setting. It is within society that the self is created, therefore the self can best be understood through understanding it in its natural context, society. We turn now to a description of contemporary American society and its hand in the creation of the *"default" model of the self.*

Notes

1   Walt Whitman's *Leaves of Grass* (1855, 2000) is a great poetic declaration of expressivism, to take a couple of examples: Do I contradict myself? Very well then, I contradict myself, I am large, I contain multitudes." "I celebrate myself, and sing myself, and what I assume you shall assume, for every atom belonging to me as good belongs to you."

2   For example, German priest Martin Luther (1483–1546), and the greater Reformation, which provided the context of the German understanding of the self, claimed that Reason is a whore and thus God cannot be understood through the intellect.

3   Catharsis in this context is a term made famous by Sigmund Freud. A sentiment encapsulated in the following quote: "Pleasure becomes a crucial means of recognizing that ideal truth and beauty which imagination reveals … and thus becomes the means by which enlightenment and moral renewal can be achieved through art" (Campbell, 1987, p. 205).

4   Rieff describes four character types in western culture: political man, religious man, economic man, and psychological man. Psychological man repudiates religious man by living beyond conscience and negates political man by exhausting Liberalism.

5   See Janov (1970).

6   See, for example, Lasch (1979).

7   From "Below the Surface-stream." First published in "S. Paul and Protestantism II," in Cornhill Magazine, November 1868.

8   See Whyte (1960).

9   Also note the likeness between consumer, Freudian, and Christian guilt.

Chapter 4

Consumer Society

T he second part of this book focuses on consumer society and marketing since the self is the intersection of the type of society we are a part of and the meaning and values we create for ourselves. The structure of society, albeit distorted by the distribution of wealth and power, represents and molds the needs of its constituents. In contrast to the first part of the book, which described *why we buy*, the second part of the book is an exploration of contemporary American society as a consumer society, that is, of *how we buy* and how it came to be this way, in other words, the social determinants of the self in its societal context. Chapter 5 provides a focus on advertisements: where values meet consumption. In Chapter 6, I elaborate an analytical framework for advertisements in America, France, and Egypt to compare the relation between the *"default" model of the self* and consumer society within different societies.

This chapter provides a description of how and why America is a consumer society by exploring its historical, sociological, economical, and cultural bases. While agreeing that the "consumer (is) someone engaged in a 'cultural project', the purpose of which is to complete the self" (McCracken, 1988, p. 88), my own further main claim is that in the consumer society that is contemporary America, consumption has come to function as a platform for the creation of meaning and values for an individualist and expressivist self.

The following selective description of the pertinent history of consumer society in America will help us to better understand the structural causes behind our present systems of values and the *"default" model of the self*. Two strands in the relation between the self and consumer society to focus on in the following narrative are: the political shifts toward individualism dramatized in the balance between public and private spheres, and the shift towards personal expression through consumer goods.

I. Consumer Society

Consumer society has a history of approximately three hundred years and caused a nonreligious revolution: it changed every feature of social life (McKendrick, Brewer, & Plumb, 1982; Lury, 1996; Glickman, 1999). It led to no less than a new definition of the person and her relationship to society; a new form of social orientation and values for social action (McCracken, 1988, p. 25). The emergence of the consumer revolution coincided with the Industrial Revolution (1750–1850) in that the latter necessitated a correlative demand for consumer goods. Some important developments of the consumer revolution in the eighteenth century that are still apparent today are: a new definition of the person and of desire; the participation of subordinate classes in consumption; a rise in the importance and ubiquity of advertising; the sophistication of marketing; the obsolescence of goods; and a shift in the symbolic properties of consumer goods that came to assume a gate-keeping role for social mobility (McCracken, 1988, p. 21). Over the next two hundred years, consumption of goods overlapped with, then slowly became the foundation of, expression in social life; it became a vital component in social subsistence.[1] This state of affairs is referred to as "cultural frames for goods" by some authors and refers specifically to the set of values and forms of communication that exist in the interplay between marketing, mass media, and popular culture (Leiss et al., 2005). As a way of characterizing epochs in consumer society, this approach represents the relation between persons, goods, and images of well-being as they are represented in advertising: "idolatry" (1890–1920), "iconology" (1920–1950), "narcissism" (1950–1970), and "totemism" (1970–1990).

As we proceed, some definitions are in order. First, goods are items on the commercial market designated for sale. A commodity is a type of good that has value. Value can be broken down into two subtypes: exchange value, what other goods the commodity can be exchanged for, and use value, the utility of using a good. Consumer society and consumer culture will be used interchangeably.

Broadly speaking, what are the main characteristics of consumer society, and how do we know which societies fall under this designation? One key element of consumer society is that people who live in a consumer society formulate their goals partly through acquiring goods that are not needed for material subsistence or traditional display. Goods include basic material necessities and also "positional goods" that place us in relative social standing (Hirsch, 1976). According to historian Gary Cross (2001), consumer society has no formal philosophy, leaders, or parties, but has come to be successful because it is a concrete expression of the cardinal political ideals of the century—Liberalism and democracy. In this way, consumer society has partially replaced civil society by creating new networks for emotional and social outlets.[2] Consumerism is able to serve as a proxy for Liberalism insofar as it possesses notions of individual rights, self-directed institutions, political pluralism, unrestricted markets, and a limited role for the State; consumer society gives meaning and dignity to people when labor, ethnic, and representative democracy have failed as cohesive forces (Cross, 2001). It reinforces participation and equality by making liberty not an abstract right to public discourse but an expression of oneself through deliberate acquisition decisions and a realization of personal satisfaction in and through goods in daily experience. The expressive individualism of dynamic mass society allows emergent societal groupings, which give people the means to establish, or assume, their own identities. An important social consequence of the acquisition of goods was that it allowed individuals in the subordinate classes to challenge traditional social stratification based on landholding and noble lineage (De Vries, 2008). In many ways, the promise of a democracy of consumers co-opted and restructured prevailing notions of class identity (Cross, 2001).

According to sociologist Celia Lury (1996), the relation between the self and contemporary consumer society is characterized by a strong belief that "to have is to be," wherein self-identity itself becomes a possession. In this schema, consumer society provides the conditions for a politics of identity. The connection between self-identity and these notions of acquisition and possession is the focus of this chapter: "[I]t is precisely as expressions, creators, and innovators of a range of cultural meaning that goods have contributed to the rise of the modern West" (McCracken. 1988, p. 10). With the emergence and solidification of consumer society in the twentieth century came an increasingly reflexive relation to self-identity as a form of self-fashioning. To a large extent, it is in acquiring, using, and exchanging things that individuals come to have social identities in a consumer society. Consumer goods function as bearers of social meanings; in some cases they act as banners of consumer group identity. As early as the eighteenth century, the cultural meaning of goods was a way for members of a densely populated, and therefore anonymous, urban society to maintain social familiarity with those one sees on a day-to-day basis:

> Consumers now (in a developed consumer society) occupied a world filled with goods that carried messages … they were surrounded by meaning-laden objects that could only be read by those who possessed a knowledge of the object-code … more and more social behavior was becoming consumption, and more and more of the individual was subsumed in the role of the consumer.
>
> (McCracken, 1988, p. 20)

In the extensive 30 years of literature on consumer society, the two main explanatory structures for *why we buy* are producer-led and consumer-led. An example of the former is Karl Marx's idea that fetishism of the material product is a process of reification where labor becomes alienated and the product functions as a substitute for labor. An example of the latter is Modern Euro-American societies, where high intensity market settings train individuals to be consumers.[3] Although the following partial historical account of consumer society in America does not emphasize the tension between different sectors of society throughout the rise of consumer society, strong currents of dissent were always, and continue to be, prevalent.[4] My own argument focuses on producer-led political shifts toward individualism dramatized in the balance between public and private spheres and consumer-led shifts toward personal expression through consumer goods.

II. The Historical Origins of Consumer Society in America

1880–1930[5]

Following the Civil War, a secular business and market-oriented culture with exchange and circulation of money and goods at the foundation of its aesthetic life and moral sensibility grew out of the prevailing urban and rural capitalist system. Important features of this culture included acquisition and consumption as the means of achieving happiness, a quest for the new, the democratization of desire, and money being viewed as the measure of social value (Leach, 1994). The spread of consumer desire to most of society had roots in democracy, while the "cult of the new" subverted traditional values and folk ideas. A diffusion of comfort and prosperity became the centerpiece of the American experience, and was institutionalized as equal rights to desire goods and enter a world of comfort and luxury; this vision took over from the Jeffersonian vision of agrarianism, republicanism, and religion.[6] Consumer culture emerged with the help of a new set of commercial aesthetics and practices (e.g., advertisements and promotional bargains), collaboration between economic and noneconomic institutions (e.g., community associations and community merchants), and the growth of a new class of brokers (e.g., distributors). The core aesthetic of all these groups was a vision of the good life and an earthly paradise of consumer goods (Leach, 1994).

After 1895, stores, museums, churches, and government institutions acted together to create a society that depended upon a redirection of aspirations toward consumer longings, consumer goods, and consumer pleasures (Leach, 1994). As a response to a rapid fall in prices, high labor costs, intense competition, and market volatility, large business corporations superseded mid-nineteenth-century firms by basing their business model on high volume, full capacity production, and domination of mass markets. Corporations (i.e., legally recognized social organizations marked by administrative hierarchies, managing technologies, and controlled labor created to generate capital through private and public stock ownership, and to manipulate market controls in order to make profit [Galbraith, 1958]) sought to end competition through gaining control over prices, labor, and middlemen (Leach, 1994). America was the first country to have an economy devoted to mass production and mass consumer institutions (Lury, 1996). One element of this economic and sociological transformation was the growth after 1895 of the so-called service industry, that is, an industry that provides nontangible services to businesses and customers; these services include accounting and leisure industries. Through the guiding logic of awakening consumer desire, merchandising, department stores, and the concentration of resources through incorporation manifested the values of pure comfort and relaxation. Consumer service also separated the world of production from the world of consumption; this separateness helped transform consumption into the true realm of freedom and self-expression as well as the refuge for comfort and pleasure (Leach, 1994). There came a resulting need to diffuse desire throughout the entire population so that the surplus of goods created by concentrated production and sold through merchandising and department stores could be consumed. Fashion merchandising embodied this quest for the new. For example, the new fashion journals *Vogue* (founded in 1892) and *Cosmopolitan* (founded in 1886) through representations of models for a host of desired values, gives consumer goods a value over and above their intrinsic worth thereby imbuing them with special desirability; fashion merchandising lifts consumers into a world of luxury beyond work, drudgery, and the everyday humdrum; it also stirs up restlessness and anxiety in a society where class lines are blurred or denied (Zola, 1883; Tiersten, 2001).

Beginning in the last decade of the nineteenth century administrative wings of the Federal Government developed bureaus specialized to assist, organize, and regulate the business sector. For example, commissions such as the Federal Trade Commission (created in 1914) were created to guard the consumer's interest. Another major process wherein the Federal Government underwrote the business sector was the development of the Postal Service, which led to the construction and maintenance of roads used to anchor the transportation of goods manufactured and distributed by the business sector. Business strategies and sales promotion became standardized with the rise of an emphasis on managerial organization. For example, advertisements took on their own stylized cultural language with a hook and a pitch. Other important institutional changes caused by the nascent corporate power structures of early consumer society in America were easy credit starting in 1922, the development of installment plans, charge accounts, small loans, and credit policies to make up for inequity in incomes. In 1932, the Commerce building was opened in Washington, D.C., by Herbert Hoover (who was the Secretary of Commerce from 1921–1928 before his tenure as President from 1929–1933), it was the biggest office structure in the world and represented a new circuitry of institutions formed to serve the interests of the business sector.

By the early twentieth century, the Federal Government became an economic catalyst that guided and intervened upon the private sector (a macroeconomic strategy referred to as Keynesianism) (Galbraith & Salinger, 1990). It was Herbert Hoover's belief that government should do everything in its power to keep the burgeoning private sector on the right track since capitalism was a moral system that led to a better humanity. The aim and function of the government thus became finding ways to balance individual and corporate desire with production and eliminate what were considered to be barriers between goods and the people (Leach, 1994). Part of this strategy included a rejection of any attempt to control the process of individual, and more notably corporate, capital accumulation. In effect, Hoover reinforced and promulgated an antidemocratic trend in American politics and economics by working for the managerial elite of the private sector under a putative, some may argue misguided, vision of the benefits of industry for the well-being of all members of society.

The State and the private sector intermingled in a number of ways, and the private sector became dependent on government guarantees of bank deposits and farm loans to both protect and bail it out in cases of corruption or overreaching. The legacy of this early period in consumer society in America are still apparent: for example, the private sector relies on the Postal Service (a government-built and supported institution), while federal monies educate workers for employment, immigration policy provides cheap labor, and federal and state governments generate vast amounts of demographic census data that is used by the private sector. While these consequences of the early period of consumer society in America have positive ramifications for civic society, they are also available for use, not to say exploitation, by a private sector that does not have to answer to a voting public. Starting in the early-twentieth century there has been a trend, which is stronger now than ever, wherein government institutions serve the business community (Leach, 1994; Chomsky, 1999; Cohen, 2003).

In terms of urban infrastructure, after 1885, spaces for consumption often functioned as community social centers and overlapped with churches for members. By 1910, department stores served as anchors of downtown civic life, acting as the main public spaces for citizens to congregate and live their daily lives (Leach, 1994; Cohen, 2003). As a consequence of these transformations, older social controls were weakened by industrial expansion and community integration was effectively disrupted; a new capitalist culture filled the void. Consumer society arose when a rural and traditional society was transformed into a mass industrial population. Fordism—an early twentieth-century producer-led industrial strategy characterized by mass production, centralized management, labor movements, and homogeneous commodities—paved the way for mass production and growth in national markets across social class (Ewen & Ewen, 1992).

In summary, the origins of consumer culture in the late-nineteenth and early-twentieth-century were: 1) the maturation of the national marketplace, including the establishment of national advertising, 2) the emergence of a new stratum of professionals and managers rooted in a web of complex new organizations (e.g., corporations, government, universities, media, etc.), and 3) the rise of a new gospel of therapeutic (i.e., expressive) release through relaxation and luxury preached by a host of writers, social scientists, doctors, ministers, and advertisers (Lury, 1996).

1930–1980

The main characteristic of this period in consumer society was a blurring together of democratic and business values in public and private policy, which led to a correlative shift from citizenship to consumership. This process was made possible by a shared commitment on the part of policymakers, civic groups, the business sector, and labor leaders to put mass consumption at the center of a prosperous postwar America (Harvey, 1989). Post-Fordism is America's late-twentieth-century consumer-led industrial strategy characterized by flexible, specialized production, globalization, a large service sector, and a heterogeneous range of products (Ewen, 1976). Post-Fordism has the social consequence of creating a new middle-class characterized by social scrutiny and class positioning based on acquisition of consumer goods. This led to the growth of fancied needs of marginal utility, for example, fashion and style. These fancied needs create conditions conducive to an excessive concern with the expressive possibilities of consuming goods for the self, a self-fetishization. The expressive rather than the functional/instrumental use of goods was emphasized; one's consumption of a lifestyle was the definitive mode of social communication. Consumers display their individuality and *taste* through their choice of consumer goods. Lifestyle embodies the ideal manifestation of a new social consciousness in pursuit of expression and individuality; it expands identity into a social context (Leiss et al., 2005) and provides a fundamental means for individuals to seek meaning, identity, and stability (Giddens, 1991). For British sociologist Celia Lury (1996), consumer choice has become the means by which our society thinks about individual agency and makes judgments about personal identity. This is highlighted by Lunt and Livingstone's (1992) empirical findings, which demonstrate that consumer culture infiltrates everyday life at the level of economics, social life, and meaningful psychological experience.

Between 1930 and 1980, the notion of a "citizen" was co-opted by the notion of a "consumer" when the focus of society became safeguarding the general good of the nation and protecting the rights, safety, and fair treatment of individual consumers in the private marketplace. Citizenship itself has a storied history and has shifted in relation to its influence on government representatives and then individualist rights in relation to the rise of judicial powers after 1937 (Schudson, 1998). During the early and mid-twentieth century, as part of an individualist shift, citizen-consumers were urged to contribute to society by exercising purchasing power and not by asserting themselves through political influence on government representatives. These changes were most clearly observed in the New Deal (1933–1936), which sought, and established, permanent representation of consumers in the government. This way of empowering the consumer enhanced the public's stake in a society based on the free enterprise system. Public works job programs and progressive tax policies inspired by economist John Maynard Keynes in the 1930s made consumer-citizens responsible for higher productivity and full employment, a responsibility that was formerly fulfilled by producers. During World War II, private and domestic tasks became civic and political within the context of consumer society when consuming was considered patriotic because it kept the economy, and thus the country, afloat. It was also during this period that preference for private market solutions that would boost the mass consumption economy—even if they had to be heavily subsidized by the government—over more statist solutions turned a dire social need for, for example, shelter, into an economic boon, as seen in the public housing and the "condoization" of urban space (Cohen, 2003). Until the mid-1960s, political efforts aimed at gaining equal access to mass consumer markets would prevail over alternatives that challenged the economic and cultural status quo more fundamentally. In fact, part of the goal of the Civil Rights Movement (approx. 1950–1980) was for African-Americans to have access to mass consumption, and part of the sympathy they aroused across the country was from this desire to be a part of the marketplace (Cohen, 2003). Keynesianism, as well as consumer credit and borrowing, made consumer demand the centerpiece of a prosperous postwar economy; the American citizen became redefined as a purchaser whose economic behavior, rather than protecting the rights of individuals in the marketplace, supported the general good through fueling aggregate demand (i.e., the total amount of goods and services demanded in the economy at a given overall price level and during a given time period).

In terms of urban infrastructure, between 1947 and 1953, in a domestic transformation referred to as white flight, the suburban population increased by 43 percent. This "segregurbia" made racial mixing less prevalent in the suburbs.[7] The suburban home became what

American historian Lizbeth Cohen (2003) called Consumer Republic's quintessential mass consumer commodity as it was capable of fueling the fire of the postwar economy while also improving the standard of living of the mass of Americans. The suburbs had a built-in socioeconomic stratification that dictated where and how one lived—home pricing served as the most obvious class sorter in the segmented postwar metropolitan housing market. Regional shopping centers (or malls) emerged as a new form of community marketplace in the late-1950s. At first, they were built along highways to be reached by car, but then they were built to replace urban town centers in the busiest thoroughfares in the suburbs themselves. The major lasting effects of regional shopping centers are the commercialization, privatization, and feminization of public space (Cohen, 2003). These shopping centers served a civic function as well; through careful site selection, marketing, and policing necessary for control, they became an idealization of downtown without vagrants, rebels, minorities, and poor people. In the new public space of the regional shopping center, consumption, luxury, and leisure were inseparably intertwined, thereafter constructing community experiences around the cultural tastes of white middle-class suburbanites. These areas were zoned as self-taxing Business Improvement Districts (BID) and supported by urban merchants to compensate for inadequate government attention; through this process they became free of municipal oversight and public accountability. For some critics, dependence on private spaces like shopping centers for public activity and privatization of public space through BIDs re-zoning threatens the government's constitutional obligations to its citizens. Supreme Court Justice Marshall in 1972 made the following statement concerning these domestic changes:

(C)ities rely more and more on private businesses to perform functions once performed by governmental agencies … as governments rely on private enterprise, public property decreases in favor of privately owned property. It becomes harder and harder for citizens to communicate with other citizens … Marsh v. Alabama holds that "the more an owner, for his advantage, opens up his property for use by the public in general, the more do his rights become circumscribed by the statutory and constitutional rights of those who use it."

(quoted in Cohen, 2003, p. 277)

As a result of this unfettered pursuit of profits, the new metropolitan landscape was largely privatized and segmented. This made precarious the shared public sphere upon which democracy depends (Cross, 2001). The less shared space citizens have, the less reasons and ways they have to come together and be affected by the same things, the less the population may achieve a united political voice.[8]

In the 1950s, the market was explicitly segmented by social class and retailers developed strategies to fill particular niches in the marketplace based on age, income, education, geography, and ethnicity. According to Cohen (2003), segmenting the mass market helped bring more of the population into consumer society because submarkets were shaped around the priorities of each demographic. At the same time, this customization led the political motivations of citizen-consumers to be co-opted because the reification of social difference in the pursuit of profits helped cement economic inequality and existing power relations were not altered.

President Dwight Eisenhower's 1952 and 1956 campaigns brought mass marketing into the political arena, thus pricing political office out of the range of all but the most affluent and powerful citizens. Furthermore, political leaders were pushed away from appealing to a shared political agenda by the market segmentation approach. Any discussion of the common good was avoided in the interest of serving the specialized interests of distinct constituencies. The legacy of this element of consumer society in America is that voters have come to expect the political marketplace to respond to their narrowly construed needs and interests while issues of the general good are ignored. America's ongoing residential stratification and privatization of public space made broad-based political agendas difficult to construct and maintain. For politicians, consumer rights served as the universalizing liberal alternative to racial and gender rights talk in the 1960s. This rhetoric and legislation offered an inclusive discourse about the exploitation of consumer rights in place of the more divisive industrial-era discourse about the exploitation of labor and economic inequality (Cohen, 2003).

Policies launched by President Gerald Ford (1974–1977) were embraced by President Jimmy Carter (1977–1981) and expanded upon by President Ronald Reagan (1981–1989); these include the deregulation of the economy and a diminution in the authority of the Federal Government through a weakening of regulations and moving critical government functions into the private sector (Reich, 2007). Consumer-citizens related to the government as shoppers in a marketplace, and their greatest concern became, 'Am I getting my money's worth?' Public institutions, through competition and deregulation, were presented in such a way that consumers were urged to think and act toward them like individualist stockbrokers bent on getting a better deal, meanwhile the business sector had little to no accountability. Keynesianism was replaced by Reaganomics, which substituted supply-side policies for demand-oriented policies. Tax cuts, cuts in government spending, the elimination of entitlement programs, and an anti-inflationary money policy won the day in the 1980s. Promotion of capital investments, concentrated wealth, tax cuts, and personal savings over consumption functioned under the misguided assumption that prosperity would trickle down. In reality, the inequality of income grew enormously such that the top 1 percent now had more assets than the bottom 95 percent combined (Reich, 2007). The search for profits and the exigencies of the market prevailed over the higher goals of liberalism related to political democratization for all members of society. This resulted in a decline in voting and a decline in putative democracy.

In summary, in the place of town squares, Americans are now left with commercial spaces strongly influenced by the private sector and often stratified by race and class. This results in a narrowing of common ground and a retreat from concern with the general good. Cohen (2003) concludes that common and public goals should derive from a broader understanding of the diversity of the nation's population, because such a broader understanding would make room for citizens who are not primarily defined by their relation to consumption. But this state of affairs becomes more distant as the economic behavior of consumption becomes more entwined with the rights and obligations of citizenship and social orientation becomes more individualist (Giddens, 1991).

1980–Present

During this period, consumption became a means for fulfilling personal fantasy; affluence tipped the balance away from discipline and toward hedonism. Due to its need for limitless spending to sustain growth, capitalism undermined the very discipline that created prosperity in the early-twentieth century (Cross, 2001). The general problem, according to American cultural historian Gary Cross, was a lack of willingness to forego gratification and contain desire within the boundaries of the home and the family, and one's own means.

In his two terms of presidency (1981–1989) Ronald Reagan transformed regulators into deregulators and weakened consumer protection and shared social services by turning public interests over to the market (i.e., "privatized" public services). The more wealthy Americans became, the less willing they were to be taxed for services they thought, or were increasingly convinced by Reagan-era propaganda, they were using less often (Lilla, 2010). The savings rate sank despite fiscal policies, while consumer debt rose. Tax cuts in 1981 led to greater income and salary inequality, and huge increases in defense spending led to a reduction, or privatization, of public services (Krugman, 1997). These private/public partnerships initially seemed mutually beneficial but soon turned into private control behind a philanthropic façade. Moreover, private sector sponsorship of a wide array of festivals, sporting events, and celebrations has led many to feel that creativity and congregation are impossible without the involvement of the private sector. At the same time, commercial speech came to be protected just as much as religious and political speech, paving the way for further privatization of public space through billboard advertisements (Klein, 2001). Social stratification continued with the development of gated communities within the suburbs. Meanwhile, consolidation in the business sector expanded, for example, department stores grew into huge retail centers—Superstores—peddling an enormous variety of goods at low prices made possible by cheap foreign and domestic labor. When the Federal Trade Commission (FTC) lost its regulatory bite under President Reagan in the 1980s and antitrust laws were weakened, powerful corporations able to conglomerate and multiply avenues of control through synergy and quasi-immunity from the law were created (Klein, 2000). One of the consequences of the corporate striving for profit has been the booming service sector, which as of 2001 made up 75 percent of total employment in America. These part-time jobs are characterized by perpetual transience, a lack of social mobility, and a disposable workforce with no representative labor organizations to oppose the dictates of management. Meanwhile, within the gainfully employed class, the Yuppie (Yuppie is short for the young urban professional class; they are characterized by conspicuous consumption) subculture developed, it combined radical individualism with perpetual hard work toward acquiring domestic luxuries (like personal computers) and a more prolific concept of choice in regard to consumer goods and leisure activities (Leiss et al., 2005).

The last 30 years also saw a rise in celebrity culture wherein people compare themselves to celebrities rather than to their neighbors (Klein, 2000). The fantasy world of videogames for isolated children and teenagers gained in popularity, while shopping itself came to be considered a form of entertainment (Norton, 1993). These shifts between reality and fantasy—between private and public spheres—led to a blurring of the line between entertainment and advertising. This ambiguity has also seeped into the division between public relations and education. The difference between the mall and the museum as entertainment and the collection and accumulation of goods nearly disappeared. Furthermore, new avenues of consumption in the "experience" or leisure industry arose, for example, widely available forms of tourism, the availability of esoteric or obscure collectible goods, and the proliferation of cultural activities (Cross, 2001). It is fair to say people became separated from their communities as consumer goods fulfilled their social needs more conveniently.

Shifting to an individual conception of pleasure in the private sphere impeded political participation because active democracy requires cooperation between large groups of people who do not know or necessarily trust each other (Cross, 2001). Civic health is measured by voting participation, social trust, social membership, quality of public discourse, the disparity between rich and poor, the capacity of the least advantaged citizens to be heard in the political process, and the reach of state-guaranteed rights (Schudson, 1998). Subsequently, the negative consequences of consumerism for many critics fit into two categories: personal/interpersonal and institutional/political. In regard to the latter, consumerism drove out social concerns in its individualist social orientation, a relation to the past in its quest for the new, and obligations for the future in the availability of credit and the permissive culture of hedonism (Fox & Lears, 1983). The political Left now celebrates expression and difference while the political Right celebrates markets and narrow moral concerns. As we enter the twenty-first century, both politically and personally we are faced with the possibilities of unbounded opportunities for consumption with no alternatives.

Cultural historian Gary Cross urges Americans to establish boundaries to consumer markets by moderating needs and legislating consumer rights. Ultimately, abundance should mean more than the plenitude of commodities (Lears, 1994). Americans bear the responsibility for the social and personal costs of consumerism, which include a culture of self-isolation and an undermining of the sense of collective responsibility necessary for a successful democracy. In addition, this transformation in social orientation leaves little space for social conscience or tradition; by placing the focus on individualist wants, public goods are undermined by the market system (Cross, 2001). Private corporations have become more than just purveyors of goods, even though they are not held to the same accountability controls as public institutions, they are now the most powerful economic, and many claim political, forces in the nation (Klein, 2001).[9] Cross (2001) attributes the success of consumer society to its victory over other systems of values. Consumer goods became markers of status, participation, identity, progress, and memory; they gave shape to life transitions. They worked so well in meeting immediate needs that Americans did not conceive of other options that may have been as satisfying, and critics had no realistic social and economic alternatives that balanced personal and social needs in one cultural system.

Finally, the cultural and economic changes that constituted the rise of consumer culture brought about changes in the political structure of the democratic state. Consumable democracy emerged as the natural expression of American industrial production; the liberty to consume became equated with political freedom. Democracy was treated as if it flowed out of people's needs and desires as an expression of the people's ability to participate in consumption (Ewen, 1976). These individualist transformations have proven detrimental to the functioning of a successful participatory democratic system.

In summary, the key characteristics of late-twentieth and early-twenty-first-century consumer society were compulsive spending, a leisure industry, apolitical passivity, a permissive morality of individual fulfillment, and a consumption-oriented society dominated by private sector bureaucratic organizations (Lury, 2006).

With this history in tow, let us turn to the connections between contemporary American consumer society and the *"default" model of the self.*

III. The Counterculture, Liberalism, and Consumer Society

The shift of expressive possibilities from public to private spaces highlighted in the preceding partial history of consumer society in America comprises the driving force behind the twentieth-century critique of consumer and military-industrial society known as counterculture.

A key episode in the recent history of American consumer society was the Counterculture Movement of the 1960s and early 1970s. The expressive individualism of this era was a culmination of a trend toward using goods, rather than personal relationships, to define the self (Cross, 2001). The Countercultural Movement (approx. 1960–present) resulted in a widening of the range of avenues for expression and was ultimately a product of social changes in advanced industrial societies where material plenty enabled people to look beyond immediate necessity and make serious aims out of expressive needs such as self-discovery, exploration of the personality, and deep personal relationships (Martin, 1981). Cultural historian Jackson Lears (1994) characterizes this spiritual and psychological climate of consumer society as "the new gospel of relaxation." It reflects a culture where self-realization—doing away with social masks so as to allow the authentic self its autonomy and ultimately manifest one's individuality—is viewed as the highest aim of human existence and experience itself is prized over its goal. Jansson (2001) claims this Romantic ethos is just one of many modes of consumption. Consumer culture functioned as a value system and new set of sanctions, it replaced Protestant salvation with therapeutic self-realization

(Lears, 1994). Yet this total freedom of the authentic self was in tension with the other goal of the counterculture: total community, getting along with each other, and sharing (Martin, 1981). A dramatic byproduct of this tension was an undermining of traditional moral bedrocks: as emotional fulfillment became the sole avenue for self-realization, the "new gospel of relaxation" led to a decline of symbolic structures outside the self like the nation or the church. In consequence, there was a devaluation of public life in favor of a fantasy leisure world of intense private experiences.

Philosophers Andrew Potter and Joseph Heath (2004) see consumption as integrated with social identity; they link consumer society to expressive individualism in that Americans consume goods that confer distinction. The essential ambiguity of goods in this relationship is fundamental to their malleability of meaning and infinite appeal (Martin, 1981). In this portrayal of consumer society, competition, not conformity, is the problem; people identify with brands because of the distinctions they confer such that distinction drives consumption rather than the desire to conform. Contrary to their goals, counterculture's critique of mass society has ended up being one of the most powerful forces driving consumerism in the past 50 years because it is always renewing itself to be against the culture (Potter & Heath, 2004):

> At its core consumerism stems from the belief that goods both express and define our individual identities. When consumerism is combined with a cultural obsession with the quest for authentic self-expression, the result is a society collectively locked in a large number of consumption traps. Because of our further conviction that fashion is a superior form of expression, that clothing has a language of its own, it is not hard to see why the relentless fashion cycle has become the dominant locus of competitive consumption.
>
> (Potter & Heath, 2004, p. 185)

"Cool" is the central ideology of contemporary consumer society—it is a positional good, a distinction-based manifestation of *taste* (Gladwell, 1997). Being "cool" derives its value from comparison with others; it is individualist in that it seemingly liberates individuals from the shackles of society (Potter & Heath, 2004). "Cool" replaces class, which was based on the Protestant and bourgeois values of material wealth, productive work, social stability, and respectability, as the central social position marker (Potter & Heath, 2004). In a capitalist economic system, anyone can make money, so mere wealth is not sufficient to define the social elite. That is where "cool-ness" usurps the class system and becomes a determinant factor in the social positioning of individuals within society. Cool-ness is visible on the surface and ultimately depends upon consumption.

For Potter & Heath (2004), countercultural rebellion ends up being a set of dramatic gestures devoid of progressive political consequences but nevertheless providing a source of contempt for democratic politics. The counterculture has helped further the rhetoric that shared governance structures are an artificial imposition invented by a powerful elite that have nothing to do with them.[10] It has helped separate public and private spheres and consolidated expressive individualism as legitimate and "cool-ness" through *taste* as the predominant mark of social standing. This sentiment against democratic institutions was a factor in the lack of attachment to the public sector demonstrated by citizens during the privatization of the public sphere that began in the 1970s.

According to sociologist Bernice Martin (1981), expressive individualism had the consequence of splitting lives into specialized role-playing within large and impersonal institutional structures. This splitting of life generates two sectors, labor (or work) that places a high value on rationality, calculation, and efficiency, and leisure that consists of self-fulfillment, spontaneity, and experiential richness (Bell, 1976; Bellah et al., 1996). The political scientist Anne Norton in *Republic of Signs* (1993) claims that since the labor sector of life is a coercive system of subordination, Americans are forced to turn to leisure for their freedom and political power. Outside the workplace, citizens in a consumer society have inalienable rights to exercise choice; whereas production is a system of constraints, consumption is an exercise of freedom, not only in acquiring things but also in the representation of sentiments and self. Consumers transferred moral and spiritual values to the more intimate private sectors of life, thus devaluing customs and traditions designed to preserve cultural memory and family continuity. Historically speaking, the quest for self-fulfillment during leisure time compensated for the loss of autonomy in the post-Fordist workplace (Lears, 1994). Consumer society offers an alternative avenue for self-determination and self-expression that is absent in the workplace. Consumer goods can serve as signs of class, regional provenance, race, gender, ideology, religion, occupation, the causes one supports, etc. "People (who) realize themselves via consumption not labor rely on commodities to satisfy their needs and desires … they require choices to answer their need to constitute their own identities and reveal themselves to the world … (It is) in the use of commodities as a system of representations that capitalism is assimilated to democracy" (Norton, 1993, p. 51). The profusion of goods thus expands the expressive possibilities of the self. These consumption practices assert not only self-expression but also mastery over social structures within which the consumer is embedded. Consumers transform consumption from a necessity to a source of pleasure and an assertion of power over the world. This exercise of self-determination through consumption as individual expression is at the core of Liberalism and contemporary capitalism. For example, Norton discusses how in the act of consumption, minorities and women (i.e., those who lack access to the press and power in general), through their semiotic sophistication in the marketplace, interject themselves into the public discourse. Norton thus connects consumption practices in America to the central ideals of Liberalism in that choice in the marketplace represents freedom. The freedom of *taste* is manifested as the autonomy to select how one represents oneself to others in society. Leiss et al. (2005) consider the cultural frame of goods in contemporary times to be what they call "mise-en-scène": a demassifying process where consumers use goods as props in creating and re-creating value and shared meaning. In this way, the consumer can shuffle elements of personality to achieve satisfactory social grouping and role-playing forms of identity as a lifestyle. This shows the power of representation through consumer goods in that within a consumer society, *taste* functions as a social communication that defines the self to others. Furthermore, insofar as public space is structured around consumption and the political characteristic of the *"default" model of the self* is individualism, citizen-consumers regard the autonomy to consume as the praxis of democracy. In summary, consumer society engages our central political and personal needs—autonomy, democracy, and self-expression—in a way that is accessible, personalized, and immediately gratifying (Potter & Heath, 2004). We turn now to the way that *taste* functions to connect the self described in the first part of the book to consumer society.

IV. The Culture of Consumption: Taste and Style

As described in Chapter 3, *taste* is an expressivist manifestation of the individualist inner self, and therefore living a particular lifestyle, within a consumer society, is manifesting one's authentic, or inner, self. A cultural phenomenon that is important for understanding the relationship between consumption and the self is *style*: the way human values, structures, and assumptions are aesthetically expressed and received (Ewen, 1988; Bourdieu, 1984). Style provides a powerful means of expression by encoding and transmitting social values and ideas deeply rooted within historical codes for values and meaning. Style is unique in that it is defined by its consumption and its value in the immediate cultural circumstances; it is thus a perishable item linked to the ability of the mass media to convey popular notions of style (Wernick, 1992). Style is also an element of power woven into the fabric of social, political, and economic life, in that certain groups and individuals are able to shape it and certain stratifications are fabricated to structure the field of meaning. According to author Russell Lynes (1949), the history of *taste* as a form of social consumption can be broken down into three ages: 1) Public taste—when the upper class tried to discipline higher appreciation for arts and sensibility into the middle and lower class; 2) Private taste—when the elite furthered their own aesthetic interests by acquiring collections and commissioning works; and 3) Corporate taste—the age of mass culture. Practically speaking, style is an intimate component of subjectivity in that through investing consumer goods with meaning it intertwines people's aspirations and anxieties and functions as a visible corridor between the world of things and human consciousness. With this concept of style we can see that mass production actually provides individuals with the tools of pre-conceived identity. A culture of abundance serves as a provocative, though passive, definition of participatory democracy, in which though the power of the upper classes remain unavailable, the symbols and prerogatives of the influential class in a given society are made available to the masses. This notion that each individual has access to status and recognition, and therefore can escape anonymity and attain a state of belonging within a clearly constructed consumer group, is tied to the American belief in democracy. The American economist and sociologist Thorstein Veblen's (1899) concept of conspicuous consumption expresses this state of affairs as how people express their personalities in consumer goods and tend to buy things that symbolize their aspirations for others to see. In contemporary consumer society, mass-produced stylized goods function as a kind of identity kit, a palette of symbolic meanings, which are psychological essences (Ewen, 1988). Accordingly, Roland Barthes (1972) defines a "fashionable person" as a bricolage of stylistic elements combining to present the semblance of an integrated subject. In this way, the self can be considered a commodity in the social marketplace (Sennett, 1978). The utility of style is thus to provide evidence of socially understood meaning in one's life; it is the key element of an absorbing social masquerade. Style is the way in which people display their individuality in a consumer society that is an arena of social dialogue of desires expressed symbolically through mass-produced and mass-marketed consumer goods.

Let us now return to the concept of *taste* introduced in Chapter 3 in relation to expressivism and the self, this time in the context of the social structure of consumer society put forward thus far this chapter. In the sociologist, anthropologist, and philosopher Pierre Bourdieu's scheme (1984), *taste* is a marker of one's position in society because cultural preferences are the product of social origins and education, and aesthetics cannot be disconnected from cultural knowledge (Gans,1974). Bourdieu claims that since *taste* functions as a marker of class, the act of consumption is a process of communication. People are distinguished socially by the cultural distinctions they make, class is therefore apparent through the specific aesthetic points of view on everyday choices and common objects that people take. Each class is defined by both intrinsic properties and relative position in the class system. A given person's cultural dispositions constitute his *habitus*. "*Habitus* organizes ... perception of the social world and is itself the product of internalization of the division into social classes" (Bourdieu, 1984, p. 170). *Habitus* functions below the level of consciousness and language, and is therefore beyond will and introspection. Lifestyles can thus be defined as differences in the ability to differentiate, appreciate, and appropriate distinctions in the cultural world; they are the social symbol of *habitus*. *Taste* then is the generative formula of lifestyle, as it transforms consumer goods into social and cultural signs. "The cognitive structures which social agents implement in their practical knowledge of the social world are internalized, embodied social structures" (Bourdieu, 1984, p. 468). Values thus become apparent in the most automatic gestures. They are the product of the incorporation of the fundamental structures of a society; these principles of division are common to all agents of society and make possible the production of a common meaningful social world within a consumer society.

In summary, in American consumer society *taste* seems to function as an expression of the authentic self. This chapter provided a historical description of the social determinants of this inner self, a thoroughly natural entity in the social arena of consumer society.

Summary

This chapter recounts a partial history of consumer society in America and highlights key themes in this transformation of society related to the *"default" model of the self*. These strands were connected to the socially conditioned markers of *taste* and *style*, naturalizing the self as a product of its social and cultural conditions. An important task remains: where can we look to see where values and meaning are explicitly represented in American consumer society? The answer, explored in the next chapter, is advertisements.

Notes

1 Consumer society as "cultural frames for goods" is most convincingly described in Leiss, Kline, Jhally & Botterill (2005). This traditional history has recently been challenged by the narrative of an "industrious revolution" by De Vries, J. (2008). *The industrious revolution: consumer behavior and the household economy, 1650 to the present*. USA: Cambridge University Press. De Vries argues the consumer society arose out of changes in the organization of labor within the household. The excess value thus created made possible the purchasing power, availability, and acquisition of goods in the market.
2 Adam Curtis's "The century of the self" (2002), BBC films, makes a similar argument.
3 For good compendiums on these issues, see *The consumer society reader* (2000). Juliet Schor (Editor), D. B. Holt (Editor), Douglas Holt (Author), The New Press: USA. And, *Consumer society in American history: a reader* (1999). Lawrence Glickman (ed.) Cornell University Press: USA.
4 See Schudson (1998), Breen (2004), and Zinn (2009), as well as many other titles in American History on Seven Stories Press.
5 American historians of consumer society, for example, Lears (1995), generally view 1880 as the beginning of a distinctly American consumer society.
6 See Etzioni (1998) for a contemporary call for moving back toward roughly Jeffersonian values.
7 This was even institutionalized in certain areas, for example, see *Redlining: discrimination in residential mortgage loans* (1975) created by the Illinois General Assembly, Legislative Investigating Commission.
8 See conclusion.
9 See the conclusion for more on issues facing us in the twenty-first century.
10 Even though the twentieth century has shown that sometimes people are served better by following a centralized set of rules. This libertarian rhetoric continues in the Tea Party movement of 2010, see Lilla, M (2010). The Tea Party Jacobins. *The New York Times Review of Books*. May 27, 2010.

Chapter 5

Advertisements: Representations of the Self

dvertisements are the most direct and prevalent way we come into contact with the underlying values and motivations of a consumer society in our daily lives. If you are not at home while reading this, take a look around, how many advertisements do you see? According to an article in the *New York Times*, the market research firm Yankelovich estimates that a person living in a city 30 years ago saw up to 2000 advertisements a day, compared with up to 5000 today.[1] Contemporary advertisements are not passive either; slogans and jingles echo in many of our social practices as reference points and have come to serve as a common cultural lexicon. Advertising provides us a bank of current cultural meanings. Take, for example, "Have you had your break today?" or "Just do it."[2] These advertisements have become memes, cultural ideas transmitted and spread like genes across the population according to selective pressures. Advertising is the mediation of human needs through consumer goods; it is an institution that currently stands as the most influential form of socialization in contemporary society (Jhally, 1987, p. 1). Advertisements reflect many values in our society more accurately than anything else (Henry, 1963), they integrate the consumer within a rich and complex web of social status and symbolic meaning wherein consumption serves as a ritual to make sense of the inchoate flux of society and culture (Douglas & Isherwood, 1996).

The aim of this chapter is to provide a description of how advertisements in contemporary America achieve a large part of their success in providing people a way to concoct meaning by appealing to the *"default" model of the self*. The chapter begins with a partial history of the marketing industry behind advertisements. This is followed by an explanation of *semiology*, a method of reading the signs and symbols used in advertisements. S*emiology* is then couched in the context of culture, a mode of analysis referred to as *mythology*.[3] Finally, a *semiological* analysis of advertisements leads me to propose a *mythology* of symbols and signs used in advertisements related to the *"default" model of the self* described in the first part of the book.

I. A History of the Industry

A partial history of the advertising industry in contemporary America will help us contextualize the relationship between desire, need, and the self in consumer society.

The American cultural and intellectual historian Jackson Lears in *Fables of Abundance* (1995) traces the history of advertising in America back to its initial strategy of standing as a symbol for the glorified unknown, which, in the sixteenth century was represented by the tradition of ever-shifting surfaces in the Carnival. Lears claims that an important element in the establishment of marketing was that pieces of paper (as novels or banknotes) could be used as floating symbols that could be harnessed within any system of meaning. The shifting surface of meaning made possible the distribution of messages from producers to consumers; it was aided by the anonymity of urban living and the fast-talking carnival-esque figure of the proto-advertiser—the peddler. Over the last couple of hundred years, advertising went from face-to-face selling messages to the repetitive printed advertisements of early newspapers to the dynamic mass communication of radio and television, and the personalization of messages via cable, Internet, and direct mail. "It is a story of sellers struggling to find the best means to attract buyers, and a parallel story of the public's reception, resistance, amusement, and annoyance" (O'Barr, 2010, p. 2). In effect, advertisers created powerful images of human subjectivity that embodied the values of the emergent social system (Lears, 1995). Advertising plays a role in the pervasive language of the therapeutic ethos, the "new gospel of self-realization," rooted in America's feeling that selfhood had become fragmented, diffuse, and unreal because of a range of factors: urbanization, technological innovation, the rise of interdependent economies (which implies a loss of individual control), the secularization of liberal Protestantism among the educated and affluent, and the anonymity bred therein. Advertising was successful in its early incarnations because it was able to respond to these disorienting changes associated with modernization and present products as magical solutions to the alienation of modern life (Lears, 1994). Advertising was also an institutional resolution to the problem of how to reach consumers in an industrial, urban society (Pope, 1983). In a way, modern advertising is simply a more streamlined manner of stabilizing market relations through representations and solidifying the fit between the preferences of consumers and the world of organized competition for success.

We now turn to a history of marketing and advertisements in America vis-à-vis its relation to citizens and public institutions, that is, as an element of the consumer society we live in. The tenor of this historical narrative may appear damning overall, this is because there are a number of real negative consequences that come along with these institutions, at least that is the story reported by a large proportion of historians of the industry.

In *Adland: A Global History of Advertising* (2007), the British journalist Mark Tungate recounts how advertising hit its stride during the Industrial Revolution and the rise of newspapers as a mass medium.[4] According to the American historian Otis Pease (1958), advertisements grew in response to the needs of industrial society, which had achieved efficient methods of mass production and distribution but had not yet developed standards of consumption to maintain that production. Developed in tandem with modern commercial journalism, the advertisement industry sought to stimulate the market and create a revolution in social attitudes toward consumption (Pease, 1958). Tungate frames the history of advertising as an history of approaches, of great ideas by great men: for example, Bruce Barton the son of a preacher, advised clients to get in touch with the souls of their companies, or George Gallup, a statistician, in 1935 developed marketing research to mathematically predict the success of marketing in terms of consumption and demographics. The development of marketing was a tug of war between creatives who believed art inspires consumers to buy, and pragmatists who sold based on facts and came armed with reams of research (Tungate, 2007). The advertising industry got a real boost with the effort to secure volunteers for World War II and during the Great Depression, this was when sex began to be used in advertisements to make the hard sells for products that were not necessities during the austere times of war (Sampson, 1974). American historian Merle Curti (1967) sees the history of advertising in terms of shifting notions of human nature: from rationalistic conceptions up till 1910, irrational conceptions from 1910 to 1930, and a shift to behavioral sciences up to the postwar years. Leiss (1976) describes a shift from explicit to implicit statement of values and lifestyle images through the course of the twentieth century. Cultural theorist Sut Jhally (1987) offers the following thumbnail sketch of the history of advertisements:

Stage 1 (1890–1920)
Advertisements are based on product utility. They are regarded as a celebration of the products of a new age, wherein the focus rests on what the products do, with a great sense of discovery in the exploration of a new world of things. During this stage, text was the dominant form of communication.

Stage 2 (1920–1940)
Advertisements are based on symbolism. The focus of advertisements moves from the worship of the utility of consumer goods to their meaning within specific social contexts. During this stage there was a slight shift from the product towards the consumer. Although the qualities of the product were described a little more abstractly, advertisements were in general focused on the product.

Stage 3 (1940–1960)
Advertisements are based on personification. The shift towards the consumer was complete; people were represented in color photographs as real rather than as symbols. Products were put at the disposal of the individual and consumers were encouraged to consider what the product could do for them personally and selfishly, the object was fetishistically depicted as acting in magical ways.

Stage 4 (1960–1980)
Advertisements are based on *totemism*, that is, they are aimed at demographics based on consumer lifestyles. Consumer goods were treated as a natural species. Utility, symbols, and personalization were mixed and remixed under group signs, or *totems*; consumer goods essentially became a badge of group membership.

(Jhally, 1987, pp. 201–202)

An important transition in the advertising industry after 1980, when the role of advertisers changed from informing the public to persuading the public, was that the aim of the research sector of advertising agencies began isolating groups of people for the purposes of designing therapeutic pitches to clusters of people for each product. This is called psychographics; it refers specifically to dividing consumers based on their innermost fears, desires, prejudices, attitudes, and beliefs. In the adman-turned-author William Meyers's popular book *The Image-Makers* (1984), we find a description of how, for the purposes of marketing, society may be broken down into types of consumers. Each of the types have their weaknesses and deep-seated emotional needs that can be tapped into by making consumer goods appear as a means of soothing those emotional preoccupations. Meyers describes how the company SRI International developed a Values and Lifestyles index (VALS) dividing American society into five basic groups: Belongers (i.e., those that feel they belong and achieve a fairly stable status of comfort; this category includes one out of three Americans), Emulators (i.e., those in search of identity in the adult world), Emulator-Achievers (i.e., successful materialists), Societally Conscious Achievers (i.e., those whose consumption is within the context of greater political issues), and Need-directed (i.e., people who are poor and are only able to consume what they need). Belongers seek self- esteem and togetherness, Emulators seek self-confidence, Emulator-Achievers seek status, Societally conscious Achievers arose as a reaction to selfish consumption, and Need-directed consumers only seek to satisfy basic necessities. The marketing strategy of psychographics is an important milestone in consumer society as it represents a stage in the redefinition of citizens in terms of their consumption practices. This personalization in marketing strategy depends upon individualism and the expressive needs of the authentic self in the consumer.

Social History of the Marketing Industry

In the context of consumer society, the development of marketing transformed society, culture, and the self. Historian Otis Pease (1958) describes how "it has been the task of modern advertising to persuade the individual citizen to conceive of himself primarily as a consumer of goods" (Pease, 1958, p. 1). With the rise of public relations in the 1920s, advertisements presented a portrait of life that sanctified leisure and recreation by linking them to happiness, while romantic love was portrayed as easily and cheaply acquired by purchase. Advertisements attempt to conjure up the magic of self-transformation through purchase while also containing the subversive implications of being a successful trick (Walker, 2008). By stimulating consumption, advertisements as the mouthpiece of free enterprise in America made possible an economy of leisure, abundance, and progress (Pease, 1958). They became a form of literary art and offered ritualistic symbols to evoke a dream world of desirable consumption by enabling and encouraging consumers to discover their aspirations in the symbols used in advertisements. This made the issue of how to consume a concern to everyone; in this context, advertisements became a guide to social competence and social success (Lucas & Britt, 1950).

Some important milestones were set in this period in regard to the position advertisements occupied between public and private spheres. For example, a question that occupied policymakers at this time was, is it the Federal Government or the business sector's responsibility to regulate the burgeoning field of marketing when the claims of many advertisements could be, at best, misleading? By the time of the New Deal, it was the duty of the advertisement's publisher to control the truthfulness of what it printed. Subsequently, it was the responsibility of trade associations, who proved themselves incapable of enforcing honesty laws. The FTC was developed in 1928 to sponsor a trade practice conference of publishers that could rule on such regulatory matters. But these changes were resisted as advertisers, agents, and publishers all laid the burden of regulation on each other. In 1926, President Calvin Coolidge (1923–1929), with his numerous ties to the private sector, declared government should not interfere with advertising and that the advertisement industry should police themselves. This declaration set a precedent for a future of laissez-faire policy on the part of the government vis-à-vis corporate practices in marketing. According to Pease,

> No industry in modern times attempted more effectively to manipulate the process of consumption in an economy which had constantly to increase its consumption or crash. Indeed it might further be argued that no institution had done more to circumvent the process and operation of rational thought in a free society. Surely, none of the triumphs of capitalism in the 1920s and 1930s was more extensive or significant than the triumphs of American advertising.
>
> (Pease, 1958, p. 203)

Advertisements ushered in a new kind of truth—a false statement made as if it were true but not intended to be believed, since no proof is offered, its proof becomes whether or not it sells merchandise (Henry, 1963). This sort of pseudo-truth is able to survive because governmental institutions for oversight turn the responsibility over to the consumers themselves. The consumer movement, a collection of specialized organizations, which sought to rationalize the function of buying and to strengthen the resources and position of the general buyer in a modern industrial economy, arose in the mid-twentieth century as a response to the egregious misleading information presented in un-regulated advertisements (Pease, 1958). The main problem with marketing in general and specifically in the early twentieth century that I have been describing is that advertisements did not require accuracy, reason, or logic; they only needed to be credible to consumers. In general, advertisements circumvent conscious reasoning processes by seizing upon readers' emotions and deeper values by lulling their suspicions through consciously exploiting humor, entertainment, romance, pride of ownership, fun, and prestige (Pease, 1958). Questions of both ethics and public service ceased playing any role in advertisements in the 1940s. Thus, the industry was free to decide for itself how to use its influence and offered only a partial response to the demands of the consumer movement.[5]

Taking a critical stance, professor of communications Christopher Simpson (1994) defines advertising as psychological warfare, a science of coercion that developed side-by-side military propaganda in the twentieth century and functioned through the exploitation of the cultural-psychological attributes of the populace. World War II spurred the emergence of psychological warfare as a new form of applied communication research. According to Simpson, our common experience during the War led various leaders in social science research to engage in tacit allegiance to broadcast a particular interpretation of society to the general populace. For Simpson this amounts to a nefarious alliance between government funding agencies and the business sector to purchase viewers' attention from media outlets. But selling products was not enough for this informal cabal described by Simpson. To perpetuate the status quo of power structures, they also needed to substitute, incorporate, and inculcate their values and worldview into the viewer's minds. In a way, consumers became their commodity and values became their language.

The role of the media is important because contemporary mass communication serves as a foundational space for democracy. As professor of media studies M. P. McAllister (1996) puts it, media is different from other industries; its importance is due to its potential contribution to democracy. A media organization serves the public interest insofar as it serves the whole society and not just a part of it. In this way media is important because democracy cannot work without as much of the populace as possible being informed. For this purpose, media must be understandable as well as accessible economically and geographically. Furthermore, to fully represent the citizens, the content must also be diverse in its use of cultural and social voices (McAllister, 1996). All the while, the content must be engaging. An ideal media would serve as the prime vehicle of the public sphere where different social positions could gather to voice positions with no single voice dominating, it would articulate the public good. According to McAllister, the media should provide public spaces where public discourse in the public interest develop the ideal of the public sphere, for with a perfect media system, true participatory democracy will be more likely to occur. In practice, media is currently understandable and profoundly engaging, but what we get in engagement we seem to lose in accuracy of information and diversity of voices. For example, not a single news daily has been introduced nationally in nearly a century (McChesney, 2002). The two main problems caused by concentrated conglomerate media are hypercommercialism and the subsequent denigration of media's role as a public service (McChesney & Nichols, 2002).[6] This state of affairs reigns because media has few incentives to serve the democratic process; in fact, media corporations are designed to make money, and therefore the profit motive drives content decisions. The fuel that powers the engine of the media is advertising, not the public good (McChesney, 2002). Furthermore, to the detriment of serious analysis of political and civic issues, all messages in the media are delivered beside the flashy and engaging entertainment of advertisements. In effect, advertising's ubiquity has given private corporations the loudest voice in society; it is a voice that generally does not align with the voice of the public's greater interests (Bagdikian, 1997). The consequences of the media element of consumer society will be discussed further in my concluding chapter, although it is important to note that big media is not the whole story; there exists a rich tradition of radical media criticism, which some authors argue *is* the mainstream tradition of a free press in America. This radical critique of commercial journalism if positioned as the mainstream position in United States free press theory depicts its rival, the media in the context of free market forces, as not really "a tradition so much as a set of assumptions that has migrated into conventional wisdom" (McChesney & Scott, 2004, p. 7).[7]

Recent Strategies in the Advertisement Industry

Marketing is about mastering the grammar and syntax of commercial persuasion in the cultural lexicon of a given society. Journalist Rob Walker's incisive *Buying in* (2008) places consumerism in relation to the meaning humans need; he claims objects only matter because of their relationships to other people and larger ideas. Few stronger emotions exist than the need to belong and make meaning. Brands are poised to exploit that need and do so successfully because ultimately "we find value and meaning where we have created it ourselves" (Walker, 2008, p. 260). Consumer society is a societal arrangement wherein meaning resides in the social relations between consumers and consumer goods (Appadurai, 1986).

In general, choosing among products depends on price, quality, and ethics. Alternatively, the advertisement industry in the last twenty years has focused on developing the phenomenon of branding, the goal of which is the creation of difference in the context of a narrow range of actual differences in commodity attributes. Branding is the process of attaching ideas to products: the brand is a shorthand form of identity that solves the problem of consumer choice changing decisions traditionally based on price, quality, and ethics, into decisions based on symbols, identity, and meaning (Walker, 2008). Walker describes the "eternal dilemma" of contemporary American consumers as the desire to feel like individuals but also to be part of something bigger than oneself, just like the goal of the counterculture discussed in Chapter 3 is pure individualism and pure community. Within this "eternal dilemma", marketing blurs the line between branding and everyday life through "desire codes" that resolve the tension by allowing the creation of community through inclusion into brand tribes (i.e., *totemism*) (Sahlins, 1976). For Walker, brands and logos acquire symbolic meaning that plays a role in the psychological well-being of the consumer; he argues that the days of mass culture are over and that now companies must provide personalization such that it is the customer who is in control. In this scheme, successful products fit into disparate personal narratives by way of disparate rationales (Walker, 2008).[8] Successful brand products tell stories to others, in line with Thorstein Veblen's concept of conspicuous consumption, brands frame consumption in terms of representing oneself to others. Furthermore, successful brands create narratives for one's self, they help us make sense of ourselves in the inchoate flux of society and culture by anchoring our personalities in consumer goods.[9]

Advertising is currently best understood as the stylization of emptied-out goods. French-born American cultural anthropologist Clotaire Rapaille (2006) explains how these emptied-out goods are filled up with what he calls the culture code; this is similar to the explanatory approach I will be presenting farther along in this chapter. Culture code is the "unconscious meaning we apply to any given thing ... via the culture in which we are raised" (Rapaille, 2006, p. 5). A consumer's understanding of advertisements depends on the meaning she learns within her culture—the cultural unconscious—that functions as a referent system. Every culture has a cultural referent system of archetypes and codes that is an extension of the biological scheme; "the biological scheme identifies a need, and the cultural scheme interprets it within the parameters of a particular culture" (Rapaille, 2006, p. 93). For example, according to Rapaille, the American culture code for love is false expectation while the French culture code for love is refinement of pleasure. Rapaille's somewhat simple analysis of culture codes does not sufficiently characterize the values that drive consumption. In the next section I will describe how *semiology* (i.e., the study of symbols) and *mythology* offer a deeper understanding of how advertisements work in the context of creating meaning for the self within a consumer society.

II. How to Read an Advertisement: Semiology

An advertisement is successful when it convinces a consumer to purchase a product. As we saw earlier, selling a product through a brand depends upon selling its symbolic meaning and its social identity. These characteristics of a product are embedded in the symbols used in the advertisement (or in the product itself). For the semiotician Varda Langholz Leymore, V. (1975), each of these symbols mobilizes a set of values. To convince consumers, successful advertisements must therefore be a manifestation of the core values of a culture in symbolic form.

So how do these symbols, or signs, work? The many representations of advertising are reducible to an underlying structure: strategy (i.e., organization of the message), code (i.e., values engaged), and *mythology* (i.e., underlying ideological structure) (Leymore, 1975). Advertisements can be deciphered by the study of signs: *semiology*. In *semiology*, the *signifier* is the form that a *sign* takes, while the *signified* is the concept represented by that *sign*, together they form a *signification*; the *sign* itself has no intrinsic meaning or value independent of the context in which it is presented. The meaning of a *sign* depends on the code within which it is situated; this code provides the framework within which a given *sign* makes sense. The code unifies the different elements of the process of meaning construction because it is the store of experience from which both the advertiser and the audience draw to construct meaning through consumer goods (Jhally, 1987, p. 140). Codes are systems of related conventions in specific domains, they organize *signs* into meaningful systems, which in turn correlate *signifiers* and *signifieds*; they link sets of texts together into interpretative frameworks (Chandler, 2004). There are different kinds of codes, for example, social codes that consist of language and bodily codes (i.e., body language). There are also textual codes, which are written systems of meaning; they include science, aesthetics, and rhetoric. There are interpretative codes that are perceptual ways of interpreting what comes into our senses. Finally, there are ideological codes, which relate to the encoding and decoding of texts. Ideology refers to the "isms" (e.g., materialism, fascism) that motivate and underlie the drift of the message. Each *sign* has a literal meaning, which is its *denotation* and a set of sociocultural and personal associations that constitute its *connotation* (Chandler, 2004). For French literary theorist, philosopher, and semiologist Roland Barthes (1972), denotation is at the level of language while connotation is at a deeper level of meaning called *Mythology*.

Signs and codes are generated by *Mythology* and in turn serve to maintain *myths*. *Myths* are extended metaphors that help us to make sense of experiences within a culture; they express and serve to organize shared ways of conceptualizing within a culture. This sense of the concept *myth* comes from structural anthropologist Claude Levi-Strauss who described how the myths children are told form a fundamental system for their subsequent understanding of the world; the views and standards associated with a *myth* shape the codes that define the way we interpret the world (Leach, 1989). The ideological function of a *myth* is to naturalize the cultural; to make dominant cultural and historical values, attitudes, and beliefs seem to be entirely natural reflections of the way things are. This is an example of the first type of *myth* important for our purposes: *ontological metaphors* that associate activities, emotions, and ideas with entities and substances. The other type of *myth* is *structural metaphors* that have the overarching function of allowing us to structure one concept in terms of another (Chandler, 2004). For Levi-Strauss, all *myths* are the same *syntagm*, that is, position of elementary constituent segments within a text, or orderly combination of interacting *signifiers*, which form a meaningful whole within a text. *Syntagms* operate on an unconscious level and exert an influence on our behavior (Leymore, 1975, p. 126).[10] *Mythology* mediates between abstract and concrete as well as between social values, cultural symbols, and ordinary everyday behavior. *Mythology* is a communication process, an intersection of communication in signs and values; it uses the dialogue of *signs* to effect the exchange of values. *Myths* act as anxiety-reducing mechanisms by restating essential dilemmas of the human condition and offering solutions to them within the context of an advertisement. Advertisements, therefore, have two faces: a surface level (the visual and textual advertisement itself, i.e., the *sign*) and a hidden level (the deeper contextual framework, i.e., the *myth*), which underlies the surface representation and endows it with meaning.

In a modern industrial consumer society, advertising relies upon *Mythology* to function successfully. Not surprisingly, a society based on an economy of mass production and consumption has evolved its own *myths* in the commercial sector (Leymore, 1975, p. 156). For Jhally (1987), capitalism weakens other institutions and derives its power by providing meaning that is not available elsewhere, its power stems from the human need to search for meaning in symbols; consumer society provides these values in the world of consumer goods. Furthermore, Jhally claims consumption is the mode of living of modern culture, so that if goods are ritual adjuncts and rituals make visible and stable the categories of culture, then advertisements and the meaning they provide are indispensable for the stability of consumer society. Therefore, consumption's "real ideological role is not to create demand … it is to give meaning, that is why it is so powerful" (Jhally, 1987, pp. 196–197). In the influential essay, "Advertising As Capitalist Realism," sociologist Michael Schudson (1984) claims advertisements follow a set of aesthetic conventions that link political economy to sets of values that are celebrated and promoted through images and tropes that simplify reality, provide social models to emulate, and demonstrate optimistic progress in a capitalist future; according to Schudson, advertising is capitalism's way of saying 'I love you' to itself. Capitalist realism promotes the individualist social orientation that satisfactions are invariably private rather than collective.

Below is a formulation of how the *"default" model of the self* as a set of values serves as its own *myth* in American consumer society, how it can structure our world, and why it is important for social status and symbolic meaning.

III. Myth and Advertisements

For semiotician Judith Williamson (1994), *myths* structure the meanings of the symbols present in advertisements such that "advertisements are selling us something else besides consumer goods: in providing us with a structure in which we, and those goods, are interchangeable, they are selling us ourselves" (Williamson, 1994, p. 13). According to Leymore (1975), the fundamental goal of advertising is to communicate the deep message (i.e., the *myth*) to the viewer and its efficacy depends on its success in that endeavor.

Judith Williamson ingeniously combines *semiology* with Sigmund Freud's formulation of dreams to suggest advertisements contain a surface meaning (i.e., manifest meaning, or *sign*) and a deeper real meaning (i.e., latent meaning, or *myth*). Williamson (1994) views every image as a *signifier*, which leaves the possibility for a latent meaning under its manifest meaning. In this scheme, each advertisement functions within a referent system such that the referent always refers to the actual thing in the real world, to which a word or concept points.[11] Although the product has no meaning initially it is given value through the *structural metaphor* of a person or object, which already has a value to us (Williamson, 1994). After the product is given meaning by another object, the product may create its own meaning and change from a *signified* to a *signifier* (i.e., from the meaning of a *signified* to a *signifier* toward another, deeper, level of meaning). At that point, the product becomes the reference so that associations and emotions are generated not by connection to the other images in the advertisement but by the consumer good itself. After the consumer good achieves the status of *signifier*, it becomes a type of currency, a link between the buyer and intangible social values and symbolic personal meaning. For example, a celebrity like

Donald Trump is a *signifier* of the social and symbolic value of wealth and a successful corporate career. For Williamson (1994), this constitutes a meta-structure where meaning is not just decoded within one structure but also transferred to create another structure of meaning. Now, two systems of meaning are involved, the referent system and the consumer good's system. We transfer the meaning of the *signifier* to the consumer good; this transference may be translated by millions of people in the same culture (Williamson, 1994). "A system of meanings, a referent system, is used in its entirety to give significance to the product. And since the product cannot have a place in a pre-existing system, its link with the referent system is provided by an intermediary object that both belongs within the system, and is also tied to the product" (Williamson, 1994, p. 106). Systems of meaning, or referent systems in effect form the body of knowledge, or cultural lexicon, from which both advertisers and audiences draw. Mass media advertising thus plays the role of a mediator since for the audience to properly decode the message, advertisers have to draw from the audience's cultural lexicon, then transform this material into a message through appropriate formats and shaping the content in order that the process of communication to the audience be successful and complete (Hall, 1980, quoted in Jhally, 1987). Williamson claims:

> [There is a] basic equation in all advertising: it establishes an identity between two social "products" which originally belonged to different orders of social life but have become exchangeable through their co-partnership in signification—people and things. People become signified by, and then summarized by, things … (P)eople are the sum of their consumer goods. We recreate ourselves every day, in accordance with an ideology based on property—where we are defined by our relationship to things, (to) possessions, rather than to each other.
>
> (Williamson, 1994, p. 179)

Williamson conjures the anthropological concept *totemism* to elucidate the relationship between self and the *semiological* transference of meaning. *Totemism* means the subject becomes the *signified* or, "if the connection between the product and the objective correlative person or thing is made by us and in us, it is also made with us, in that we become one of the things exchanged (i.e., given the status of an object)" (Williamson, 1994, p. 45). The advertisement seeks to make us embody ourselves in the product, to be what it will allow us to achieve. In effect, choosing one product over another defines you since it represents your assimilation into, and acceptance of, a particular group, thus manifesting your *taste* through consumption. *Totemism* for Levi-Strauss is using differences between natural objects to differentiate between human groups; it is the universal tendency to divide nature into different groups of species and things to correlate with differentiations in the social world of people (Jhally, 1987). We identify ourselves with particular items with which we seek to define ourselves. However, the selection of these items identifies us with the image that is being sold. Rather than being differentiated by class, advertising seeks to differentiate us by the things we buy: what we buy reveals our *totem* and beneath that our *taste*. In this way consumption functions as a process of individualization. According to the philosopher and political scientist William Leiss (1976), commodities have this transformative power because they are collections of characteristics, or symbols, rather than sets of product qualities. Commodities are highly complex material-symbolic entities since consumers order preferences in terms of characteristics of objects; they assimilate objects into the social world. In a sense we are created by what we buy. By automatically associating *myth* and ideology within a product, we give that product meaning. In turn, by buying a product, we create ourselves in the image that we gave it, thereby assimilating ourselves into the product. The buyer must already feel a part of it before he buys it—it is what makes an advertisement speak to us (Williamson, 1994). We turn now to elucidating this connection between the self and consumption through the mediation of advertising.

IV. The *Myth* of the *"Default" Model of the Self*

Humans are social animals; therefore in a consumer society consumption is intrinsically a social activity. Since the social process of making and acquiring meaning in contemporary consumer culture is mediated by advertisements, we should be able to read the values of a society in its advertisements, a sort of spectator ethnography. If a successful advertisement sells a brand and selling a brand is selling meaning and identity, then it should be possible through the use of *semiology* to formulate a *mythology* of meaning and identity that explains the success of any given advertisement in a particular culture. Consumer goods and advertisements sell us tools for the construction of self. Advertisements not only reinforce society, they also reflect it and contribute to cultural discourses. In the symbols that define and represent products in advertisements we find who we are and what we should buy, we can also see ourselves as who we want to be through the product.[12] Advertisements communicate implicit messages about social values and carry an ideological bias toward the present societal structure by emphasizing ideas and images that coincide with the status quo; they dramatize different articulations of the American dream (Marchand, 1986; Schudson, 1984). Products sell a lifestyle and it is up to the consumer to use these products to achieve that goal. We distinguish ourselves (and position ourselves in *totems*) through the products we most relate to, and through these decisions based on our *taste* we construct ourselves via this *structural metaphor*. We are given the illusion of freedom and participation to actually interpret the advertisement; "as though the jigsaw piece is defined by its surrounding pieces, so is latent meaning of the advertisement to its constituent signifiers" (Jhally, 1987, p. 78).[13]

The first part of the book provided a robust characterization of the self in contemporary America through a description and explanation of its three main aspects: metaphysical dualism, individualism, and expressivism. I contend that this characterization of the self accurately represents a *myth* of the *"default" model of the self* upon which the value and meaning of a large proportion of advertisements in contemporary America depend. This *myth* of the *"default" model of the self* provides the metaphysical, personal, and practical aspects of the self—the core values of the self—within contemporary American consumer culture. I hypothesize that the values encapsulated in this *myth* are what a large proportion of advertisements in contemporary America rely upon to sell products and perpetuate a consumer society.

As Figure 5.1 depicts, the *signifier* refers to the *signified* and together they comprise a *sign*. In this case, the *sign* constitutes the advertisement and the advertisement is in the context of an act of consumption within a society where things are bought and sold, a consumer society. Consumer society itself is the referent system where the *sign* may *denote* (i.e., have a literal meaning). Furthermore, the *sign* within the context of a consumer society only gains value and meaning through the *myth* in which the *sign* is in relation to its context. This is an ideological system where the *connotation* of meanings within their sociocultural and personal associations come into play. The *myth* is the level at which the natural is transformed into cultural meaning, which is then used as the basis for value and meaning; this is the ideological function of *myth*, to ground a particular interpretation of reality (i.e., to form an *ontological metaphor*).

My claim is that in contemporary America, the *myth* that gives many advertisements (i.e., *signs*) value, as well as social and symbolic meaning, is the *myth* of the *"default" model of the self* described in the first part of the book. Many advertisements succeed by tapping into the *myth* of the *"default" model of the self* and its value system of the expressive and individual nature of the authentic self. It is a self that is metaphysically dualist, individual,

Signifier:	X	
Signified:		Y
Sign:	Advertisement	
Context:		Consumerism
CODE		
MYTH:	*'default' model* Metaphysical Dualism Individualism Expressivism	*of the self*

Figure 5.1

and only expressive of its authentic nature through creative desire, which in a consumer society is manifested as *taste* in acts of consumption.

The only way to discover whether or not this claim is true is through an empirical analysis of advertisements. So as to better ascertain the validity of my claim that the *myth* of the *"default" model of the self* is the psychological context for the creation and perpetuation of consumer society in contemporary America, the next chapter provides the results of a comparison of advertisements from three very different sociocultural milieus.

Summary

This chapter offered a description of the history of the marketing industry and its social context. The landscape of media and advertising was depicted in the context of the social values and meanings inherent in a consumer society. Finally, a *semiological* analysis at the level of *mythology* revealed a *myth* of the *"default" model of the self* that represents the cultural basis for a large proportion of advertisements in contemporary America. The final chapter will feature an empirical analysis of this claim through a comparison of advertisements from America, France, and Egypt.

Notes

1 Story, L. (2007). Anywhere the eye can see, it's likely to see an ad. *New York Times.* January 15, 2007.

2 McDonald's and Nike slogans. Another example of this *meme* phenomenon is when an object becomes referred to by its brand name rather than its true name, for example Kleenex or Xerox.

3 Not to be confused with the more prevalent meaning of the word used to refer to folk/traditional stories. Mythology in the context of this chapter is derived from an anthropological tradition, specifically structural anthropologist Claude Lévi-Strauss (1963, 1967), as well as a semiological tradition, specifically, the work of literary theorist Roland Barthes (1972).

4 At this point it may serve us well to understand the standard structure of an advertising company: there is a creative department that consists of a copy director and an art director, there are the corporate account managers, and there is a planner who observes consumer behavior and analyzes the client's product. Media planners analyze where and when the client's advertisement should be placed, and the media buyer negotiates the purchase of advertisement space. The production department oversees realization, and deadlines, invoices, etc., are handled by the traffic department (Tungate, 2007).

5 The greatest victory of the consumer movement is probably Ralph Nader's crusade for seat belts in 1965 (Cohen, 2003). Recently, President Barack Obama's FTC's Bureau of Consumer Protection also comes to mind.

6 The global media system is comprised of several tiers; the first tier includes ten conglomerates (AOL Time Warner, Disney, Bertelsmann, News Corporation, Viacom, Sony, Vivendi Universal) which each gross ten to 35 billion a year (McChesney & Nichols, 2002).

7 This history is chronicled in McChesney & Scott (2004). Examples of contemporary public interest media groups include: Fairness and Accuracy in Reporting, Consumers Union and Consumers Federation of America. Free Press, Prometheus Radio Project, Reclaim the Media, Center for Digital Democracy, Rocky Mountain Media Watch, Action Coalition for Media Education, Commercial Alert, and People for Better Television.

8 In the case of the Hello Kitty brand, among others, consumers can construct the meaning of the brand. See the mise-en-scène cultural frame of goods (Leiss et al., 2005).

9 Cf. Neuropsychologist Michael Gazzaniga's Left Hemisphere Interpreter (see Chapter 1).

10 Different *paradigms* can change the underlying message or moral of the *syntagm* (Chandler, 2004).

11 The referent is external to the *sign* whereas the *signified* is part of the *sign*.

12 See cultural historian Roland Marchand's (1986) introduction to *Advertising and the American dream: Making way for modernity*, 1920–1940 Berkeley, CA: University of California Press.

13 See Schrank (1979) and Bourdieu (1984) on the matter of free will and consumption. Agency within a consumer society will be explored in the concluding chapter.

Chapter 6

The Rest of the World: An Empirical Test

The model of the self, taste, and consumer society in America provided thus far will remain incomplete if not set within the context of the rest of the world. This chapter provides a description of the history and pertinent sociocultural characteristics of two other consumer societies in order to provide comparison cases of the relation between self, *mythology*, and the advertisement strategies that propel consumer society. Original research that tests conceptual claims made throughout the book will be presented. Specifically, an empirical test that compares and contrasts advertisements in three cultures—America, France, and Egypt—so as to investigate the relation between advertisements, values, and the *myth* of the *"default" model of the self*. By the end of this final chapter of the book, the reader will have heard both conceptual and comparative empirical arguments for the existence of the *"default" model of the self* in America and some of the nuances of its relation to consumer society.

I. Individualism and Collectivism

In the first part of the book, in addition to psychological causes, the *"default" model of the self* in America was depicted in terms of its unique cultural roots in historical, religious, and philosophical circumstances. The social psychologist Harry Charalambos Triandis (1989) makes a related claim that culture shapes an individual's social and individual orientation, including impressing the shape of the self that has been effective in the past. Accordingly, psychologists use three continuums to characterize the possible shapes the self can take within the context of society: Individualist–Collectivist, Tight–Loose (i.e., how tight are social codes of behavior), and Cultural complexity.[1]

Individualism encapsulates the social orientation of most North American and Northern and Western European cultures, in contrast to collectivism that encapsulates most Latin American, Asian, Middle Eastern, and African cultures (Triandis, 1989). Individualists prioritize personal goals over collective goals whereas collectivists make no distinction between personal and collective goals. Furthermore, individualists are idiocentrics in that they are concerned with achievement but may be lonely, while collectivists are allocentric, which means they report less feelings of alienation and receive social support while having less individualist motivations for achievement (Triandis et al., 1988). In individualist cultures, individuals prize autonomy, independence, and self-reliance in addition to individuality. In contrast, collectivist cultures promote conformity in public settings to tradition and familial responsibility. Individualism as a set of values is said to arise in a society upon attaining greater affluence and cultural complexity:

> the greater the affluence of a society, the more financial independence can be turned into social and emotional independence, with the individual giving priority to personal rather than in-group goals.

(Triandis, 1989, p. 509).[2]

In an individualist society one has a greater number of in-groups to choose from and therefore can opt out of those in which she does not want to participate, in effect, she has looser bonds of exchange relationships. Collectivist societies, on the other hand, have tighter and more communal in-group social relationships. Subsequently, the primary concern of child rearing in collectivist cultures is obedience, reliability, and proper behavior, whereas in individualist cultures it is creativity, self-reliance, and independence.

In regard to how people conceive of their selves, social psychologists divide the self into three broad and overlapping categories: the *private self*, that is, traits, states or behaviors; the *public self*, that is, how one is viewed by others; and the *collective self*, that is, the self in relation to some collective, for example, family, or coworkers. In collectivist cultures, the *public self* is considered an extension of the *collective self*. In general, individualist cultures emphasize the *private self* whereas collectivist cultures emphasize the *public self* and the *collective self*. The self that develops in collectivist cultures is largely defined by its relations to others and is concentrated in rural areas where intergenerational interdependence secures family livelihood. On the other hand, the self in individualist cultures develops within the family model of independence, generally in an urban context, where intergenerational interdependence is not necessary for livelihood. A third category of self is developed urban areas of collectivist societies and combines the relational self with autonomy and develops the family model of emotional interdependence, where material interdependency weakens but emotional interdependence continues (de Mooij, 2004). In each type of culture there develop corresponding variants of individualism: in individualist cultures, there is vertical individualism where each person is independent and different, while in collectivist cultures, there is horizontal individualism where each person is interdependent and different. One's cultural position on these continuums influences one's relation to the world as manifested in one's behavior and what kinds of information from the world become salient when sampling, processing, and evaluating one's immediate environment. These different ways of conceiving of the self, and thus the world, have important consequences for the way society comes to be structured via the social orientation taken by the individuals that constitute the society. One way in which this becomes relevant is when we consider how a given individual creates her identity; individualist cultures emphasize the possession of property whereas collectivist cultures emphasize the role of social relationships. This research in the psychology of cross-cultural advertising largely supports my argument positing an individualist, expressive *"default" model of the self* in America.

Cultural categories concerning the self and identity provide basic guideposts for hierarchically categorizing our values. Global marketing firms use these cultural categories to understand the consumer they are selling to and connect products with the appropriate values. An insider view on global consumer behavior and marketing will provide a useful background for the empirical study of advertisements in which this chapter will culminate.

Consumer Behavior, Culture, and Marketing

A science of consumer behavior has taken shape in marketing departments and business schools across the world in order to understand, and manipulate, why and how people buy. This discipline uses cultural knowledge to better market consumer goods. The major distinction they make across global markets is between individualist cultures (where the individual is the dominant unit) and collectivist cultures (where the group, or the family, is the dominant unit).[3] Accordingly, brands in individualist cultures have to be unique, distinct, and contain consistent characteristics, whereas in collectivist cultures the brand personality should be viewed as being a part of the larger whole of society (de Mooij, 2004). Co-extensive with this split in cultures is the accompanying difference in psychological value systems. Value is an "enduring belief that one mode or conduct of end-state of existence is preferable to an opposing mode of conduct … (a value system) is (the) learned organization of principles and rules that help one choose between alternatives, resolve conflicts, and make decisions (Rokeach, 1973). Values are important in regard to how the attributes of the product influence a consumer's purchasing decision. A consumer associates the characteristics of a product with the benefits of the product, which will be liked or disliked based upon one's values (de Mooij, 2005). Value systems are generally culture-specific, for example, perseverance ranks as the most prized personality characteristic in Japan, whereas it is relatively low in the list of virtues in other cultures. Advertisements must therefore present a brand product in a way that matches how a given consumer conceives of herself in and through her psychological values. Advertisements directed to collectivist cultures stress in-group benefits like interdependence and togetherness, whereas those directed to individualist cultures stress individual benefits like independence, personal success, and autonomy.[4] In the context of this cleavage, individualist cultures brands are sculpted to possess an ideal and unique identity, whereas in collectivist cultures brands serve the need for conformity with one's social group (Hui & Triandis, 1985). Insofar as consumption can be driven by functional or social needs, marketers distinguish between formal work-related associations and informal family and friend influences upon behavior and decision-making. In addition to these factors, there are the reference group and the group toward which the consumer aspires that need to be taken into account. The science of consumer behavior further distinguishes three types of motivations for consumption: physiological, learned desires, and psychological, that is, goal-directed.[5]

But how do consumers view the products themselves? Research shows individualist Americans categorize objects on the basis of category membership and shared features, whereas consumers in a collectivist culture like China categorize objects on the basis of context and in relation to other objects and social groups (de Mooij, 2005). In collectivist cultures, information is generally acquired via interpersonal communication, whereas in individualist cultures, people in general acquire information via media outlets (de Mooij, 2005). In both cases, information is then organized by each person into a generalized narrative, that is, a script, which includes: what to do with the object, the consequences of using it, and the environment in which it is used. Individualist cultures form context-independent scripts, whereas interdependent collectivist cultures form context-dependent scripts, that is to say collectivist cultures look at the context of images while individualist cultures look for explicit messages in images (Han & Shavitt, 1994). According to de Mooij (2005), the logic of advertising in individualist cultures is: tell how the product is different, tell why the product is the best, give the consumer a justification for the purchase, and if the consumer is satisfied and trusts the company the product will be purchased again. In contrast, the logic for most collectivist cultures is: make friends with the target audience, prove that you understand their feelings, show that you are nice, build trust and familiarity; after the purchase, whether the product is good or bad will determine future consumption (de Mooij, 2005).[6]

This section traced the most important elements of global consumer marketing, namely the individualist-collectivist continuum, *private*, *public* and *collective* selves and their relation to motivations for consumption. These considerations coincide with how myths that pertain to the psychological motivation for consumption beneath the surface of the advertisement allow images to represent values; this more fundamental level will be the focus of the empirical test below.

II. Global Marketing and the Self

In the first part of the book, the *"default" model of the self* in America was described and in Chapter 5 a model was provided of how marketing, as a central facet of consumer society, advertises to Americans by appealing to a *myth* of the *"default" model of the self*. Historical, personal, and practical reasons for my argument were provided, but the empirical question of whether and how advertisements actually appeal to the self in America in relation to the rest of the world has not yet been broached. If in fact advertisements are a representation of a given culture's beliefs and desires, as argued in Chapter 5, it is essential to conduct an empirical comparison of marketing in America and marketing in other cultures to discover the veracity of claims vis-à-vis the *mythology* that is a major force that propels consumer society.

As we have seen, marketing in its global context adapts to the culture of its target audience. For a host of conceptual and historical reasons detailed below, the empirical study will focus on two specific cultures as comparison cases to individualist America: France, a developed individualist consumer culture, and Egypt, a less-developed collectivist consumer culture. The next section provides an introduction to the countries through descriptions that focus on the history of their respective consumer societies and sociocultural structures so as to better understand the psychological values that advertisements in the respective cultures draw upon.

France

Origins of Consumer Society till 1945

France serves an important role in the history of the development of consumer society because Paris was the center of the European world between the seventeenth and nineteenth centuries when mass consumption became an integral component of Western European society. It was in France in the seventeenth century that the bourgeoisie merchant class developed the wealth necessary to consume in a way that was previously only available to the noble class. It was also in Paris in the nineteenth century that the first shopping centers— *Le Bon Marché* and *Le Louvre*—and the enlightened model of consumption were most finely developed.

Early mass consumption in France was characterized by "a radical division between the activities of production and of consumption, the prevalence of standardized merchandise sold in large volume, the ceaseless introduction of new products, widespread reliance on money and credit, and ubiquitous publicity" (Williams, 1982, p. 3). Consumption in France was tied to a discourse of its cultural superiority and civilizing mission, *civilisation*; it was through consumption that French noble and bourgeoisie women demonstrated their taste in the context of modernity (Tiersten, 2001). This included a social need to exhibit consumer objects. *Civilisation* was a variation of Enlightenment ideals of art, science, and learning in society-at-large, especially as it pertained to the development of courteous and restrained behavior. Stemming from the court of Louis XIV (referred to as "the Consumer King"), the rural-based bourgeoisie absorbed an aristocratic lifestyle of consumption and leisure. The subsequent revolutionary period (1789–1815) gave a larger proportion of French society access to bourgeois and courtly consumption; luxury moved from private noble households to the public marketplace (Williams, 1982). After the revolutionary period, a new elite achieved through birth, wealth, or significant talent came to constitute a consumer class.

An important milestone in the history of consumer culture, the Paris Exposition of 1900, brought on a sea change in the way products were sold; it was the beginning of marketing by appealing to the fantasies of the consumer, a "conjunction between imaginative desires and material ones, between dreams and commerce, between events of collective consciousness and of economic fact" (Williams, 1982, p. 65). This was an important step in the development of psychological needs over physiological and learned desire needs. The wider availability of credit made possible by creditors like Georges Dufayel in the 1870s, and the proliferation of affordable goods that imitated luxury items together simultaneously democratized luxury and discretionary spending. French Historian Rosalind Williams distinguishes four models of consumption that characterized French consumer society in the nineteenth century: a) *courtly* consumption as practiced by the nobles, b) *mass* consumption for necessary goods, c) elitist (i.e., *dandy*) consumption that emphasized individuality and was tied in with spiritual and aesthetic ideas, which featured a conspicuous and imaginative display of stylized goods in the service of the construction of a unique social persona, and d) *democratic* consumption, which emphasized improving the design of ordinary consumer goods around the principles of modernity, appropriateness, and democracy so that they may have social and artistic benefits. These models of consumption are still apparent in contemporary life, as Williams notes,

> (these) lifestyles … have become dialects of a common moral language in modern society … a pseudo-moral code … lifestyles have also become a social language because people tend to seek a sense of community based on similarity in consumer habits … in these moral and social capacities, lifestyles have come to serve as guides in making choices, in setting limits, in providing traditions, in establishing reference points of individual behavior. The tragedy is that these guides, limits, and points of reference are not based on ideals of personal or social good but on the structure of power and money embodied in consumer objects.
>
> (Williams, 1982, p. 209)[7]

The first two decades of the twentieth century in France saw the rise of economic opportunities. Although the consumer economy slowed during the World War I (1914–1918), it regained strength in the interwar period before being definitively torpedoed during World War II (1939-1945) and the German occupation (1940–1944) that sunk France, along with the rest of Europe, into a terrible depression to be followed by desperate restructuring. At this point, America became a significant model and influence for how France molded its new socioeconomic consumer society infrastructure.

Consumer Society in Postwar France

After the end of World War II, many changes occurred in the infrastructure of France's consumer society as a direct result of interaction with American international outreach (most notably, the European Recovery Program, also referred to as the Marshall Plan [1948–1952]) that harbored both political and institutional goals. Robert Rochefort (1995), the head of the Center of Research for the study and observation of material conditions (CREDOC) claims the intrinsic relations between politics and economics in postwar governance redefined consumer society as the mercantile form of democracy. The international historian Sheryl Kroen (2004) documents how in the context of the Cold War (1947–1991) and under the auspices of the Marshall Plan, the practices and ideology of America's consumer republic spread to Europe. This is apparent in the transformation of

French political rhetoric throughout the latter half of the twentieth century that went from a critique of capitalism to the position that capitalism assures democracy and justice. This rhetorical and cultural transformation is far from complete, as Europe has a long and deep ideological and institutional commitment to the notion of social citizenship, enshrined in the welfare state as fostered by both Communist and Fascist leadership during the twentieth century. Also, Europe has always had greater regulations on advertising, trade, and industry in general. It boasts a longer and broader tradition of consumer cooperatives and a wide-ranging ideological rendering of consumption and its place in democracy. Notably, the use of politics in advertisements was frowned upon in Europe due to its infamous history in Vichy France and in National Socialism where it fuelled protest movements (Kroen, 2004). At the heart of the Marshall Plan was an attempt to export the new consumer practices and the political transformation of citizens to consumers of the postwar American Consumer Republic to France. These practices implied that individual prosperity and satisfaction were the barometers of the success of democracy; they were especially influential in postwar France.

Europe demonstrates a very different path of transition from a regime of scarcity and constraint after the two World Wars to one of consumer abundance in the late-twentieth century. The French historian Victoria de Grazia (1998) details the changeover in Western Europe from a bourgeois to Fordist mode of consumption; a transformation that started in the 1920s and met resistance during the mid-1930s before renewing itself based on new economic, political, and social premises in the early-1950s. The evolution of mass distribution systems accelerated in the second half of the 1960s, and by the early-1970s Western Europe had mass marketing, supermarkets, and chain retailing in abundance (de Grazia, 1998). According to de Grazia, European societies faced the challenge of responding to pressure from America to open markets as well as to recognizing the concept of social citizenship in the American way, namely as the entitlement to a decent standard of living, a condition to be achieved not by redistributive politics but in an apolitical manner by extending the means for high levels of individual consumption through higher productivity. But Europe had a different relationship between the market and the state, varying modalities of class stratification, and different notions of the rights and duties of citizens. In America, mass production coalesced with the interests of the State, large distributive trade, and consumers to achieve lower costs, regulate demand, and satisfy and shape mass tastes. This Fordist mode of organization required a total retooling of the whole circuitry of commercial mechanisms and new industries of advertising and marketing in France. But these changes were not simple since Western Europe had significantly different basic organizational elements, for example, Western Europe had protectionist barriers to safeguard small businesses, this institutional market factor was in place to protect the social order and national identity (de Grazia, 1998). Consumer citizenship in Western Europe emphasized social participation rather than individual freedom; Western Europeans sought to achieve equality of rights through economic redistribution and political organization rather than through consumer choice in the marketplace (de Grazia, 1998). France experienced a number of social changes after World War II, including rapid rates of population growth, huge urbanization, higher incomes, exposure to new products, access to credit, and new gender roles. All this reinforced change in class stratification, in particular, the rentier class transformed into the professional elite and the working class was reconceptualized as lower-middle-class salaried employees in addition to craftsmen and shopkeepers; all of these changes effectively eliminated the peasant class (de Grazia, 1998).

France had complex interactions with America over the latter half of the twentieth century when they tried to achieve the same level of prosperity and economic efficiency without inheriting its social and cultural problems. According to the international historian Richard F. Kuisel (1993), America was the background against which postwar France could define its Frenchness. This manifested itself in the changing attitude of France toward America. In the 1950s, anti-Americanism prevailed, as the French feared the social consequences of an unknown American culture, and communists portrayed American foreign aid as anti-labor and imperialist. When French dignitaries were finally sent to America in the summer of 1949, they were taken aback by the affluence of the average citizen and the difference between the standard of living of an American and French worker. They attributed this inequality to a difference in productivity, and made the adoption of American business management and institutional organization cornerstones of change in the new reconstructed French business model. The putative message of the Marshall Plan consisted of the following tenets: resist communism, abandon syndicalism, adopt free enterprise, integrate Europe economically, exert power on other countries, turn productivity of capitalism toward the consumer, future stability, prosperity, and democracy; create a practical, social, and political order like that of America in rebuilding the country after war (Kroen, 2004). The Marshall Plan was presented by Americans as the only road to democracy, it was a plan that determined how a citizen can be thought of as a consumer and how democracy can be redefined in relation to a capitalism that is turned toward consumption (Kroen, 2004). One significant Fordist institutional change consisted of giving employees equal distribution of benefits in order to raise productivity, a move that was said to push out class struggle and welcome free enterprise and market-oriented economic strategies. This strategy included shifting workers income toward consumption, it worked to such an extent that by the beginning of the twenty-first century, a French worker on average worked for only one day out of six for enough to feed a family, leaving the remainder of his salary available for consumption (Rochefort, 1995). Yet, French society in the 1950s can best be characterized as semi-collective, where social mores as well as basic life decisions largely centered on the family unit (Rochefort, 1995). Postwar marketing was singled out as one of the weakest French institutions, and thus had to be developed to take into account America's marketing strategies of making things new and creating a consumer society through fabricating need and the desire to live better through unlimited demand and easy credit. As French consumer society grew in the 1950s, the rising consumption of household goods, automobiles, and leisure and culture, were not equally distributed. Intellectuals worried about how France would survive affluence within a consumer society model that seemed to breed a mass society of conformity. While the 1960s saw an anti-American traditionalist sentiment embodied in president Charles de Gaulle (1959–1969), economic growth occurred through heavy industrialization and business mergers. As Kuisel recounts, in mid-twentieth century France,

> The benefits as well as the costs of affluence were apparent. The French now enjoyed more comforts, easier communication and mobility, greater leisure and prosperity; but they also experienced a lifestyle centered on acts of purchase, instant obsolescence, incessant advertising, a profusion of foreign companies and products, congested cities, empty villages, a faster pace of life, pollution, and the corruption of language. The discussion was now less about America and more about what was happening to France.
>
> (Kuisel, 1993, p. 186)

The generation that came of age in the 1960s was dubbed the children of Marx and Coca-Cola. Familiar critiques surfaced concerning the emotionally and creatively sterilizing effects of a consumer society based around a social order that reflected only material affluence. During this period, abundance was viewed less as liberation and more as alienation (Rochefort, 1995). The 1960s saw a transformation in the way goods are acquired; supermarkets largely replaced small retailers, retailers were increasingly referred to, and functioned as, distributors (Rochefort, 1995). In addition, there were changes to the family structure, the youth rejected sacrifices necessary to maintain a semi-collective approach, this can be seen in simple statistics, for example, meals were increasingly eaten outside of the house: 6.6 percent in 1967 rising steadily to 60 percent in 1994 (Rochefort, 1995, p. 93). The rejections of semi-collective familial social arrangements by the generation that was a part of the social uprisings of 1968 were assimilated and amplified into consumer society in the form of individualism.[8] This belies an emphasis on the *private self* to the detriment of the *collective self* and further assimilates the *public self* into the *private self*. This was evident in the rise of publicity, the segmentation of the market, and the individualization of the kinds of goods that were on the market. These changes were part and parcel of a transformation of social demographics in the kinds of jobs that constituted the economy; there was a decline in "blue collar" jobs, while the "white collar" and intellectual class absorbed a loss in symbolic prestige and financial privileges, there was a simultaneous rise of "toyotism" (i.e., lean manufacturing, lean enterprise, and lean production) as the organizational principle (Rochefort, 1995).

The mid-1980s were a period of the all-powerful consumer for a number of reasons including the eclipse of Soviet Communism and more important domestic issues like the influx of North African Arab immigrants. France became the most pro-American country in Western Europe; through the pursuit of abundance "contemporary France is a different society because of the changes associated with Americanization" (Kuisel, 1993, p. 231). But in many ways, France has resisted total assimilation and many cultural differences remain. The process of Americanization can thus best be understood as a process of selection and adaptation.

Richard Kuisel agrees with Rosalind Williams that the core of Frenchness—or the French *script*—for the French is individualism, humanism, good taste, skepticism, and above all, *civilisation. Civilisation* connotes a classical education, a refined enjoyment of life, wine, haute cuisine, a philosophical stance, and a national language that is important in itself. This sensibility is the basis of French claims to cultural superiority and is behind France's ability to be transformed by Americanization in the latter half of the twentieth century while simultaneously retaining its identity (Kuisel, 1993). Rochefort (1995) characterizes contemporary French consumer society in terms of consumption of reassurance, seen mostly in environmentally friendly, humanitarian, ecological, scientific, and healthful consumption, and the consumer as entrepreneur, wherein the immaterial desires of consumption are totally plastic and can be fulfilled in any number of ways. Rochefort highlights the following trends: an increased interest in "ethnic" products, the prevalence of tourism, and a return to the family as the central cohesive social unit, albeit whose goals are now the further accomplishments of each of its individual members.

Individualist France serves as a suitable comparison case to America and Egypt because it is a highly developed Western European consumer society with many of the same institutional markers of American consumer society but with the dissimilar values of a different social, cultural, and psychological setting.

Egypt

Origins of Consumer Society
The second culture whose advertisements will be investigated as a point of comparison is the cultural center of the Middle East. Egypt has the largest population in the Arab world (estimated 81 million in 2011), the largest military, and the second largest economy. It is the cultural leader of the region and a prominent source of Sunni religious thought (Rutherford, 2008). Egypt is an apt contrast with America and France because it has a very different economic (it is considered a third world country),[9] political (de facto dictatorship, pre-revolution),[10] and cultural (Islam) foundation than either the United States or France.[11] Egypt has an early connection to consumer society as it was occupied by France and then Britain (1798–1952). Egypt's population, however, has always had a strong set of foreign populations including the French and the British, and these occupations have left a deep sociocultural legacy.[12]

Two notable broad cultural structures, Islam and the subsequent position of women in Egyptian society, were important in the development of a consumer society. For many centuries prior to the colonial period and modern era, Muslim merchants led the world in trade, and market activity was a prominent part of city life. Islam was not hostile to material display as long as the rich paid their dues to charity. Another pertinent element of Islam is the relation between women and consumption of clothing: the practice of veiling for women did not encourage consumer display. Furthermore, Islam had pride in its unique traditional identities and so did not rush to adopt non-indigenous forms of expression. Along with poverty and the huge gap between the rural majority and urban life came an inhibition of the social need for consumer spirit and so local goods predominated but gradually in the nineteenth century, pride in European possessions developed into a sign of high status (Abaza, 2006).

From the 1890s onward, Western European firms spread in Egypt's major cities and imitative local operations followed shortly thereafter. In the early period of the decade, new consumer goods were marketed by being depicted in traditional settings. New techniques and items were inserted into the traditional site of commodity goods, the bazaar; a few department stores were also created at the end of the nineteenth century in Cairo. Credit arrangements were introduced through creditors and corollary financial institutions. A key factor in these changes was the rush of European colonial administrators and the related pursuit of oil in the region. Department stores were built in Cairo during the late-nineteenth century—the same period as they were being built in Paris—although the further social and cultural changes that occurred in France to cement and develop the practices of consumer society did not occur in Egypt for a number of reasons, including Egypt's dire socioeconomic imbalance and British colonial occupation.

In the nationalist era after 1918, many Egyptians felt divided between traditional value systems and western cultural incursions. This led marketers to attack traditional habits and selectively encourage new types of consumer behavior. Political leaders held back on adopting a consumer society because they were eager to reserve funds for industrial and military investment and also shared the anxiety over cultural change. The size of the urban middle class grew in the late-twentieth century as local and import production grew. After World War I the Middle East was inundated with films from the west; only in Egypt did a local film industry develop to share the market with western films. The influence of western movies on mass media changed the *scripts* and context relative to which consumer products were understood. It was at this point that television developed as the key marketing tool for status-conscious housewives. These changes were not always smooth as Islam has a commitment to simplicity and modesty. Since the 1970s an anti-consumerist element of Islamic fundamentalism has existed, in which rural and lower-class urban dwellers attack the urban middle class by using consumerism as a target for larger resentments against new privilege and inequality (Stearns, 2001).[13]

After Egypt gained independence from the British through General Abdel Nasser's (president from 1952–1970) coup d'etat in 1952, the state apparatus sought to provide infrastructure for the expansion of a private sector, but Nasser was rebuffed by the United States and turned to the USSR—this was one of the main factors that led to Egypt's adoption of a socialist enterprise (Abaza, 2006). Egypt under Nasser was socialist in that it relied upon import substitution and industrialization through state monopoly. Public sector companies made all the mass consumed goods in the 1950s, 1960s, and all the way into the 1980s when *Infitah* (the liberalization of the economy) instituted privatization, corruption, and the death knell of the public sector. During the putative Socialism of Nasser, sixteen families controlled intertwined political, social, and economic domains (Abaza, 2006). This sustained a large middle class that developed consumerist lifestyles influenced by both western consumerism and socialism. In the early 1970s, President Anwar Sadat (1970–1981) liberalized the economy, gearing it toward global markets and intensive foreign investment. President Sadat shifted his main foreign relations from the USSR to the west in the early 1970s, this was symbolized by his open-door economic policy of 1974, when foreign investment in the guise of the World Bank, the IMF, and American intervention led to the demise of public sector institutions, the shriveling of public infrastructure, and a sizeable amount of emigration of middle and upper class families to oil-rich countries.[14] The economic and cultural changes that took place in 1970s Egypt are known as *Zaat* (the emergence of a nouveau riche vulgar culture of quick money-making and abuse of the working class), the dissolution of trade unions, and corruption. President Sadat's reforms fomented the growth of conspicuous consumption by the nouveau riche.[15] In the late 1990s, under President Hosni Mubarak (1981–2011), Egypt, guided by international financial organizations, underwent structural changes that led to more privatization and liberalization of the economy. This, in turn, paved the way for the emergence of a new business class who further restructured the Egyptian economy away from allegiance to the Soviet Union and toward the world capitalist system (Abaza, 2001). President Hosni Mubarak consolidated the crony capitalism and monopoly of wealth begun in his predecessor Anwar Sadat's *Zaat*. In the 1990s, the sale of the public sector to private companies continued, and the private and public sector grew increasingly interconnected under the control of a new class of financiers and businessmen.

Consumer Society

In the context of the development of consumer society, all these changes in the late-twentieth century led to a reshaping of public space that merged shopping with leisure and new lifestyles of dress, technology, and architecture (Abaza, 2001). The traditional coffee shop and mosque culture of Egypt (and the Middle East, in general) is accommodating to malls as the new public space of a consumerist gentrified lifestyle. According to the Egyptian historian Mona Abaza, this burgeoning landscape of malls is a Saudification of Egypt and not an Americanization. Each mall caters to a different clientele; for example, Cairo's Bustan Centre (a multipurpose shopping arcade established in 1996) is mainly populated by middle-class housewives, students, and emerging Yuppies as opposed to the wider segment of the population that shop at the older bazaars. Furthermore, malls are beginning to include many amenities traditionally found on public streets, for example, coffeehouses and street food vendors. Demographic factors, like the 38 percent of the population that is under the age of fourteen and grew up within these new private public spaces are sure to have decisive influence on the future (Rutherford, 2008).

Abaza (2001) describes how Egypt is experiencing a process of hybridization in consumerism where global companies are transformed according to local tastes. She suggests the new public spaces of shopping malls, despite the elimination of popular street quarters and the informal sector that was ruthlessly taken over by the government and sold to private developers, may have other social consequences as malls are a space accessible to all classes. Abaza (2006) claims consumerism immunizes Egyptians from the dire political situation by detaching them from the national authoritarian policies of the dictatorship they live in. Relative to America and France, Egypt is a less-developed consumer society in that the infrastructure, economy, and culture are not conducive to the kind of involved consumer culture that flourishes in the aforementioned countries. To flesh out this thumbnail sketch of Egyptian consumer society, an anthropological view of their domestic collectivist culture is offered below.

Egyptian Social Structures

The anthropologist A. B. Rugh (1984) describes Egyptian society through its central institution, the family. The Egyptian family is an institution based on the culture's desire for belonging inextricably to a group. Family is the basic unit of Muslim society as derived from Shari'a (Muslim law). It is built around obedience, complementarity, protection, and respect; it is not built around equality, competition, and self-reliance, as are many families in western societies (Rugh, 1984). Rugh's distinction between corporate and collective social structures helps us understand the Egyptian frame of mind. Family in Egypt is a structure wherein the group comes first and individuals are expected to sacrifice their own needs for the greater good. Furthermore, the group defines the personal status of an individual first; an individual is only incidentally defined by her achievements. Individual behaviors are evaluated by how they reflect on the group such that the group takes blame or praise for these behaviors. This is different from western individualist societies, where individuals are putatively evaluated on their personal merits and can excel or fail to meet the expectations of the group without reflecting on the group itself (Triandis, 1989). In an individualist society, an individual draws on the group for support in achieving status but society holds the individual responsible for developing her own potentialities such that individual rights supersede group rights.

Rugh (1984) describes a revealing exchange with a group of young Egyptian students who claimed individualism has little positive value in Egyptian society as it is equated with negative outcomes. As one student commented: "Individualism leads to sexual license and social chaos since everyone is seeking his own ends" (Rugh, 1984, p. 34). Furthermore, "freedom in Islam implies a conscious rejection of a purely liberal and individualistic philosophy of 'doing one's own thing' as the meaning of life". The goal of freedom for the members of the Egyptian family is human creativity and freedom is defined as belonging to the community and participating with the people in cultural creation (Said, 1979, p. 74). According to Rugh (1984), this social structure sometimes leads to an inability to develop an individual sense of identity such that Egyptians see themselves (*public self*) in relation to others or in the context of their structural roles (*collective self*); religion and socioeconomic class provide membership by ascription and provide the means for social identity. Independence itself carries a social penalty in Egypt, such that self-realization is considered selfish. An Egyptian, by being a part of a collectivist society, gives up her right to equality and independence for connection and feels the sacrifice is worthwhile. By contrast, Americans can organize loosely on a broader scale without fear of larger group allegiance interfering with a disparate number of more intimate in-groups (Rugh, 1984). In Egypt, the group is the guiding light for most kinds of social and economic organization so there is little use in talking about how an isolated individual copes in his socioeconomic environment since so much depends on the backup support he commands. The individual is not the main unit of analysis as it is in America. In Egypt, the *public self* is an extension of the *collective self*. Part of what makes families cohesive is rigid complementarity of roles that are financial, nurturing, legalistic, and affective (Rugh, 1984). Family roles as opposed to public roles are the most valued social roles; individual initiative is not what counts but rather how well the person meets the measure of responsibility that family membership implies. The interests of the group and the individual within it are assumed to overlap so that social control occurs within the group and safety nets are provided by the group not by impersonal public or private institutions.

Collectivist Egypt provides an appropriate comparison to individualist France and America because it is a less-developed consumer society with a very different economic, political, and cultural setting.

Without further ado, let us turn to an empirical test designed to compare advertisements from America, France, and Egypt in relation to their underlying psychological values.

III. Global Advertisement Experiment[16]

Method

The method used herein recruits both content analysis (i.e., quantitative measurement of manifest content of advertisements) and an interpretative methodology (i.e., qualitative exploration of meaning within a given text) (Leiss et al., 2005). Although a content analysis approach by itself cannot tell us what motivates a consumer to buy, the additional interpretative methodology, in this case *semiology* and *mythology*, ferrets out the values represented in the content. Because advertisements are a relation between goods, consumers, and producer marketing, I contend that the further step of *mythology* makes this a study of the consumer's motivations for buying because it reveals the specific values that tie the consumer to the advertisement and, in many cases, to the act of consuming the advertised goods. This sort of data can also be gathered via focus groups and surveys; in this case, a *mythological* and *semiological* approach to advertisements is treated as a form of observational ethnographic research insofar as it is qualitative and investigates the cultural systems of meaning (Geertz, 1973). Although the *mythological* study of advertisements is not traditional ethnography, but rather a spectator vantage point analysis of artifacts from particular sectors of a given society, the argument put forward in this book is that within consumer societies consumption functions as a platform for the creation of meaning and values for an individualist and expressivist self and therefore advertisements are one of the means by which these meanings and values are publicly represented. In this way, an interpretative study of advertisements is a study of the values of a society, which in turn is a study of consumers themselves in a dialectical relationship with the society of which they constitute a part. Of course, advertisements are not the only reason we consume but, as argued in Chapter 5, since a significant portion of the social process of making and acquiring meaning in contemporary consumer culture is mediated by advertisements, they are a significant locus that provides us the opportunity to read the values of a given consumer society.

In this study we focus on print advertisements collected from America, France, and Egypt.[17] The magazines within which the advertisements appeared ranged along two demographics: class (broken into lower 35 percent, middle 35 percent, and upper 30 percent), and gender (is the primary target of the advertisement male or female?). The French and Arabic advertisements were translated by a translator blind to the aims of the experiment. A research assistant was trained to rate the advertisements through the following method.

Rating Methodology
For each advertisement, a general reading and overall impression of the image and copy is done, extracting the following surface-level information and assigning it a rating as follows:

- What is the brand and product being represented?
- What country is the advertisement from?
- What magazine/newspaper does the advertisement appear in, and what type of publication is it?
- What was the date of publication?
- What type of product is being advertised?

1. Drinks/Alcohol/Food
2. Perfume
3. Cars
4. Clothing/Accessories
5. Tourism
6. Jewelry/Watches
7. Electronics/Business/Telecom
8. Personal Care/Health and Beauty/Healthcare

- Which gender is targeted by the advertisement?
- What socioeconomic class is targeted by this publication?

The advertisement is then evaluated *semiologically* for its underlying messages (i.e., *myth*) concerning the self; that is to say, each advertisement is screened for elements of metaphysical dualism, individualism, and expressivism. The quantitative rubric (see below) delineates how a numerical value was assigned for each advertisement. For each element of the *myth* of the *"default" model of the self*, a given advertisement may receive a rating between 0–2; a score of "0" means there is no evidence of the element, a score of "2" means the advertisement is relying heavily on the underlying element to convey its message to the consumer, a score of "1" means there is some indication of the element. Advertisements receive an automatic score of "2" if they exhibit a strong use of the primary qualifier, as listed first under each category below.

The point system breakdown is as follows:

Dualism

- Suggestion of a spiritual dimension or soul? 0–1–2–3 pts.
- Is there evidence of a split between private and public self? 0–1–2–3 pts.
- Is there a difference between what the character is thinking vs. doing? 0–1 pts.
- Is there evidence of a self that is more personal, deep, or real? 0–1 pts.
- Does the advertisement suggest some sort of hidden mystery? 0–1 pts.
- Are the mind and the body depicted as separate? 0–1 pts.
- Does the subject display a "transcendental stare," as judged by their pose, quality of the stare, and context of setting? 0–1 pts.

Total possible points: 11
0 rating: 0–3 pts.
1 rating: 4–7 pts.
2 rating: 8–11 pts.

Individualism

- Is the individual the main element? 0–1–2 pts.
- Is the individual depicted as separate or against the group? 0–1–2 pts.
- Is there a suggestion of uniqueness from others? 0–1–2 pts.
- Is the individual shown as a judge of their best interests or displaying ownership? 0–1 pts.

Total possible points: 7
0 rating: 0–2 pts.
1 rating: 3–5 pts.
2 rating: 6–7 pts.

Expressivism

- Is there active expression through creation, activity, or body language? 0–1–2 pts.
- Is a deeper part of the character being expressed? 0–1–2 pts.

- Is there a call to action for the viewer to express him/herself? 0–1–2 pts.
- Is there an aspect of customization at play, beyond the nature of the product itself? 0–1–2 pts.
- Is there an allusion to the creation of art, imagination, or creativity? 0–1 pts.
- Is there an element of refined taste, beyond the nature of the product itself? 0–1 pts.
- Is there an element of authenticity in the advertisement, specifically the authenticity of nature, urban/inner city life, or nostalgia? 0–1 pts.

Total possible points: 11
0 rating: 0–3 pts.
1 rating: 4–7 pts.
2 rating: 8–11 pts.

Ratings were collected on one spreadsheet and analyzed descriptively and inferentially using IBM SPSS Data Collection computer program. The independent variables were date, magazine type, gender targeted, economic class, and product. The dependent variables were metaphysical dualism, individualism, and expressivism. We tested the following questions through the appropriate statistical tests (including t-tests, Analysis of variance (ANOVA), Multiple analysis of variance (MANOVA), and Analysis of covariance (ANCOVA)): Which country has the highest scores on the *myth* of the *"default" model of the self* dependent variables? Do the *myth* of the *"default" model of the self* dependent variables of the advertisements differ significantly across countries? Do they differ across class? Across gender? Do some products demonstrate the use of the *myth* of the *"default" model of the self* more than others? Do these particular products differ across countries?

Hypothesis

In accordance with claims made throughout the book, I hypothesize America will demonstrate the highest ratings on the three dependent variables that represent the *myth* of the *"default" model of the self*. Furthermore, consumer goods that are more presentational, that is, outwardly oriented, will be advertised in ways that engage the *myth* of the *"default" model of the self*.

Results[18]

621 advertisements were collected between 2009 and 2011; 241 were from America, 178 were from France, and 202 were from Egypt. Four types of magazines were drawn from: 244 advertisements from fashion magazines, 93 from business magazines, 273 from social/

tabloid magazines, and 11 from sports magazines. Social/tabloid and fashion magazines demonstrated significantly higher scores on the three dependent variables, as compared to business and sports magazines (based on an ANOVA, $p < .01$). Products were broken into social products—that is, products that are outwardly oriented—and "non-social" products. Social products are more pertinent to my hypothesis because these products necessitate advertisements that deal with psychological values, whereas "non-social" products, for example, water, are not intrinsically outwardly oriented and therefore do not directly engage psychological values. Social products had significantly higher scores on the dependent variables than non-social products (based on a MANOVA, $p < .01$). In the latter category are drinks/alcohol/food, cars, tourism, electronics, and personal care, in the former category are clothing and accessories, jewelry and watches, and perfume. The total number of social product advertisements from America was 91, from France 99, and from Egypt 86.

As hypothesized, all three dependent variables were significantly different across countries for social products (MANOVA, metaphysical dualism, $p < .05$; individualism, $p < .05$; expressivism, $p < .10$).[19] All three dependent variables also differed across gender (ANOVA totals: 317 gender neutral, 249 female target, 55 male target; $p < .05$), class (ANOVA totals: middle class 232, upper class 362, all classes 27; $p < .10$), and magazine type (ANOVA, $p < .10$).

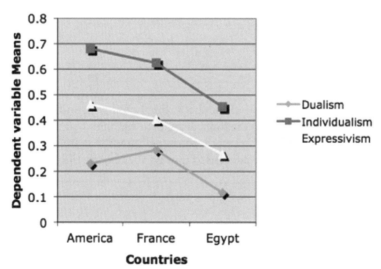

Figure 6.1

As depicted in Figure 6.1, America has the highest scores on the *myth* of the *"default" model of the self* variables, France is a close second, with Egypt far behind. Using a MANCOVA, we found that Individualism is the most different across countries and is significantly correlated to metaphysical dualism ($p < .05$) and expressivism ($p < .01$).

Conclusion

Social products demonstrate the *myth* of the *"default" model of the self* more than non-social products. The majority of non-social product advertisements only used product details and not psychological values related to the self to sell the product. It was disproportionately social products that relied upon psychological values, that is, *mythology*, in their advertisements. Consumption of social products is driven by psychological values; the empirical findings suggest the *myth* of the *"default" model of the self* is apparent in advertisements from America, to a lesser extent in France, and very little in Egypt. America had the highest scores for individualism and expressivism but not metaphysical dualism. This may be because modern dualism is the product of a French philosopher Rene Descartes, and France is historically a Catholic country. In general, France had similar scores to America, this is due to both countries being highly developed western consumer societies, and of course the influence of the Marshall Plan on France's postwar infrastructure, where possession is tethered to identity and self. This emphasis on identity is correlated with the larger range of in-groups available in individualist societies such that identity is more fluid and more amenable to influence and change, as we saw in Chapter 3, this self-fashioning is an element of expressivism. America's higher scores in individualism and expressivism demonstrate a different set of cultural values than France that would have had a higher score on the following values: humanism, good taste, skepticism, and, of course, *civilisation*. Regardless, the results validate my hypothesis that, through the use of *semiology*, advertisements—the most prominent manifestations of consumer society—in America rely upon the *myth* of the *"default" model of the self* to sell social products. In other words, *the "default" model of the self* appears to have real consequences on the way people are sold to and therefore could be considered one significant reason for *why I buy*.

The data also indicates that across countries, both lower priced items and luxury items do not rely upon the *myth* of the *"default" model of the self*, whereas mid-level products do. This is not surprising if we analyze consumer goods and their advertisements in relation to Abraham Maslow's pyramid of needs (see Figure 6.2). Product details relate directly to our physiological needs (e.g., nutrition information), and our security needs (e.g., that the car will not fall apart), while higher needs on the pyramid like belongingness, esteem, and self-actualization are more vague, they are goal-directed and relate to the social and personal meaning we create for ourselves through consumer goods. The latter needs are

© alan chapman 2001-4, based on Maslow's Hierarchy of Needs

Not to be sold or published. More free online training resources are at www.businessballs.com. Alan Chapman accepts no liability

Figure 6.2

psychological values and therefore may be approached through *semiology.* Not all products equally rely upon *mythology* in their advertisements, the *myth* of the *"default" model of the self* is most pronounced in mid-level priced non-luxury social products. Similarly, Holt (1998) found that these types of goods represented both utility as well as notions of abundance and are widely consumed across class.

The relation between shame-based and guilt-based societies is pertinent to our understanding of the results of the empirical study. Collectivist societies are shame-based since saving face and pride are the most important factors for social order; shame does not only implicate the individual but also the whole family or clan (see Figure 6.3). Guilt-based societies emphasize the individual's responsibility and negative personal response.

With respect to this distinction, individualism is the best differentiator. Egypt, with its low scores on the dependent variables and emphasis on the *public* and *collective self* is a shame-based culture, whereas France and America with their high scores and emphasis on *private self* are guilt-based societies. Both shame and guilt are apparent in consumer society, the former in terms of the social meaning of consumption (e.g., with conspicuous consumption), the latter in consumer guilt—the negative affect associated with overbuying. Consumer guilt has similarities to Freudian guilt and Christian guilt because their setting is individualist cultures where the *private self* is a crucial space for identity and values.

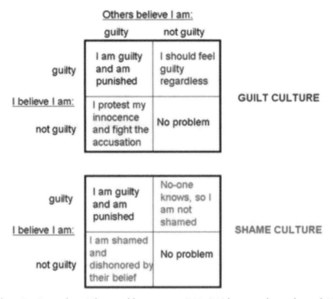

Figure 6.3: Taken from Dr. Sanity. http://drsanity.blogspot.com/2005/08/shame-arab-psyche-and-islam.html. May 29, 2011.

Summary

This chapter presents a comparison of the self and consumer society in three countries and an original empirical study, which seems to validate the book's main argument that the self in America is appropriately characterized as metaphysical dualist, individualist, and expressivist. The empirical evidence presented is drawn from a *semiological* analysis of a global range of advertisements for social products that connect with consumers via psychological values (i.e., *mythology*). It implies that the *myth* of the *"default" model of the self* is a significant factor in how advertisements work in America for social products and can thus serve as a partial answer to the question this book hopes to shed light upon: what is the relation between the self and consumer society?

Notes

1 Cultural complexity is an index of a culture's writing and records, fixity of residence, agriculture, urban settlements, technical specialization, land transport, money, population densities, levels of political integration, and levels of social stratification (Triandis, 1989).
2 In-group means a social group that shares a common fate, a common outside threat, and geographical proximity.

3   Hofstede, G. (1983). National cultures in four dimensions: a research-based theory of cultural differences among nations. *International Studies of Management & Organization* Vol. 13, No. 1/2, Cross-Cultural Management: II. Empirical Studies (Spring - Summer, 1983), pp. 46–74) also distinguishes cultures by: 1) power distance (the extent to which less powerful members of a society accept and expect that power be distributed unevenly), 2) Masculinity/Femininity, 3) Uncertainty avoidance, 4) Long-term orientation (quoted in de Mooij, 2005).

4   Acquisition centrality, that is, acquisition as the pursuit of happiness and possession-defined success in a given culture, is also an important factor (de Mooij, 2004).

5   See discussion of Abraham Maslow's hierarchy of needs below and Figure 3.

6   Marketing firms have organized their knowledge of the differences between cultures to create specific sales models. There is the *sales-response* model of the direct buy-now strategy, this is based on short-term effect and fits cultures with small power distance, high individualism, high masculinity, weak uncertainty avoidance and short-term thinking. This model works in America (de Mooij, 2005). The *persuasion* model on the other hand attempts to change the consumer's attitude and buying intention through the use of arguments. This model fits masculine cultures that have low power distance and high individualism, for example, America and Switzerland. The *involvement* model creates emotional closeness by making the brand a personality with human characteristics in the hopes of transferring those warm associations onto the brand (i.e., using *structural metaphors*). This model fits feminine individualist cultures, for example, France. The *awareness* model is based on creating awareness in order to differentiate brands; it works well in collectivist cultures that seek building trust before purchase, for example, Spain and many Latin American countries. The objective of the *emotions* model is to create a positive attitude and brand loyalty through emotions; it fits in feminine collectivist cultures. The *likeability* model is based on the idea that liking the advertisement will make the consumer like the brand. This model works well in collectivist cultures like Japan. The objective of the *symbolism* model turns the brand into a symbol, or code. This model is successful in cultures of large power distance combined with strong uncertainty avoidance as well as in collectivist cultures, for example, southern Europe and France (de Mooij, 2005).

7   Critiques of these new lifestyles in the late-nineteenth century led the Académie des Sciences Morales et Politiques in the Institut de France to engage in a series of explicit investigations of the societal changes caused by consumer society. The solutions suggested in this esteemed body included the need for reliance upon the church for spiritual matters, an extension of laissez-faire principles, a revival of Stoic philosophy, and a re-thinking of the nature of social order. Williams notes the most important critical stance was that of the morale of *solidarity* where morality is a commitment to the social whole rather than to individual needs. A parallel dialogue did not take place by a similarly sanctioned appointed body in America in response to the rise of consumer society (although see McClay, W. H. (1994). *The masterless: Self & society in modern America*. Chapel Hill, NC: University of North Carolina Press, for a discussion of the solidarity movement in America).

8   See discussion of counterculture as individualist expressivism in chapter three; the scenario in France was similar.

9 According to Mitchell (1999) in *Dreamland: The neoliberalism of your desires*. (Middle East Report, Spring: 28–33), 'the proportion of people below the poverty line increased (in the 90s) from about 40% (urban and rural) to 45% in urban areas and over 50% in the countryside" (p. 32).

10 According to Rutherford (2008), pre-revolutionary Egypt is a hybrid regime in that it is neither authoritarian nor democratic since it shares both autocratic characteristics (a powerful executive branch) and democratic characteristics like institutions that constrain the state and increase government accountability. Rutherford also notes a split between liberalism and democracy in Egypt that delineates between institutions that constrain state power and the regular holding of elections. Currently, pressures toward liberalism are strong, this might lead to a stronger private sector with autonomy from the state, which can aid democratization in a number of ways: expanding private sources of capital, strengthening protection of property rights, reducing the scope and arbitrariness of state regulatory power, and facilitating the emergence of small- and medium-sized enterprises (Rutherford, 2008). This, of course, is in the process of changing as of the Egyptian Revolution of 2011; it is unclear what political configuration will develop in the upcoming years.

11 As an economic index of culture: money spent in Egypt in 2001: food 56.1%, housing 18.7%, clothing 12.8%, transportation 7.2%, education 6%, private lessons 2.1%, sports, entertainment and culture 5.6%, health 5.3%, cigarettes 4%, furniture 3%, café and hotel 2.6%, other 3.8% (Abaza, 2006).

12 In fact, in 1910, an eighth of its population were foreigners (Rodenbeck, [1999] *Cairo, The city victorious*. Cairo: The American University Press). Even to this day, French remains the language of good manners and the upper class (Abaza, 2006).

13 This was most pronounced, and violent, in the 1979 Iranian revolution.

14 Each year, Egypt receives 2 billion in US aid (Abaza, 2006). In fact, by the end of 2006, Egypt received over $62 Billion in economic and military assistance (Rutherford, 2008). The only country that received more aid than Egypt during this period was Israel.

15 For more on Nasser and Sadat see Hopwood, D. (1982). *Egypt: Politics and society 1945–1981*. London: George Allen and Unwin.

16 This experiment took two years and involved collaboration with Jordan Compis, Hani Gabriel, Karim Gabriel, Roger Dimitrov, and Michael Haas. Support was provided by Columbia College Chicago's Center for Teaching Excellence.

17 Magazines are able to cater to specific niches and since the 1990s have been expanding in terms of advertising investment (Freeman et al., 2000).

18 See Appendix for examples of advertisements from each country and in each category.

19 We used a p-value of .10 because the dependent variables were abstract concepts, non-orthogonal, and as a strategy to raise our level of Power and avoid Type I error.

Conclusion

What Next?

W hy do I buy? By now you have read both a conceptual argument of how the self and consumer society are related in the first part of the book and an empirical analysis of this claim in the final chapter. To briefly summarize, the conceptual argument is that the *"default" model of the self* in America fulfils the social needs of identity through *taste* in the act of consumption. The satisfaction of our social needs in the microcosm of self-identity was mirrored in the slow national transformation of citizens into consumers in the late-nineteenth and twentieth centuries (see Chapter 4). In the fifth and sixth chapters, this model of the self is operationalized into the *myth* of the *"default" model of the self* and advertisements in three different consumer societies—America, France, and Egypt—are compared as to how they differentially express this myth. The results of the *semiological* and *mythological* empirical study suggest that in America—and, to a lesser extent, in France— social products are advertised by engaging the psychological values of metaphysical dualism, individualism, and expressivism. I contend that these psychological values apparent in American advertisements are a direct reflection of the *"default" model of the self*, as described in the first part of the book. This conclusion focuses on the future of the self in the consumer society of America.

Before launching into my opinion of the future of the self, it must be clarified that because the *"default" model of the self* is a historical, psychological, and philosophical consequence of the past, it is not in itself something to criticize. That is not to say that the "*default model*" is the only way the self can be structured in America, it just turns out to be the way it is currently structured. Later in the conclusion, alternative ways of conceptualizing the self are in fact suggested. On the other hand, what *are* available for criticism are the institutions that have accreted around the *"default" model of the self* and consumer society in America. It is these social, political, economic, and cultural structures that can be evaluated in the context of their effects on individual and social livelihood, as well as representative democracy. The conclusion focuses on these elements of America today, specifically the distinction between public and private spheres as raised in Chapter 4, the possibilities for subversion evident in art and activism as discussed in Chapter 3, and the skeptical and ethical question of what sorts of agency are possible within the context of consumer society.

My position is that civic engagement suffers when social relations are disproportionately satisfied through consumption. When taken as the central form of social relationships, this bond between consumption and identity ultimately endangers the community necessary for a healthy democracy. Furthermore, the waning of citizen involvement and its concomitant thinning of effective political structures, paired with the inordinate amount of civic power held by private institutions undermine the purpose of representative democracy by reducing the diversity, power, and effectiveness of the public voice. Although consumer society is the dominant structure within which people who live in a consumer society give their lives meaning, it is not the only structure capable of fulfilling this natural and necessary element of our mental health. Public and familial institutions—though greatly attenuated—remain a vibrant part of America's cultural heritage that may be drawn upon in building our identities, orienting our social behaviors, and giving our lives meaning. It is only through strengthening our extant public institutions and acknowledging community-based forms of identity and value that the self can grow past the individualist and expressivist enclosure of consumer society, however satisfactory it may appear to be in the short-term.

I. Public versus Private: Democracy in Peril

A consequence of the last approximately 160 years of consumer society in America is the re-organization of the authority of the State and the institutions of representative democracy. Both the lucrative success gained by private companies and the importance of consumption for citizens in creating meaning in their lives have led to a private sector that has more power than the public sector. The Supreme Court recently codified into law a clear example of this state of affairs wherein corporate entities are permitted to legally choose whom to sponsor in pay-to-play political elections.[1] This ruling suggests government is not an equal plane of shared governance by the body of citizens—the public. Through this ruling, small groups of people (i.e., shareholders of private institutions) who are not accountable to the public and are not liable to litigation as individuals gained, or maintained, an inordinate amount of power in financing campaigns and therefore having a say in the functioning of state and federal governance.[2] This means that domestic social ills that affect those who are not within these small groups of people—and also social ills whose amelioration is in direct contradiction to the interest of these private institutions—may not be addressed by state and federal governments.[3] The Supreme Court ruling was not a fluke or a gaff on the part of the judges, it was an accurate reflection and codification into law of how elections and the voting, lobbying, and political system work, de facto. The growth of power in private hands also has consequences for the public sphere, for example, as discussed in Chapter 5, the relative lack of public media in America limits the amount of non-privately sponsored education necessary for citizens to engage appropriately in a representative democracy. These examples demonstrate a re-organization of power detrimental to the functioning of a healthy democracy, which, ideally, represents the needs of its constituents at some sort of equal, and fair, proportion.

The consequences of consumer society—in a dialectical relationship with the psychological elements of the self-described in this book—are personal, political, and social. If the past is any indication, the longer society remains structured around consumption, the more entrenched non-public (and generally, corporate) interests become in our institutions for shared governance. If civilization is in fact interested in ameliorating social ills—such as economic inequality, a corrupt medical system, and a starved education sector—what actions remain open to us when social, political, power-relational, and psychological needs are predominately organized around the act of consumption? More specifically, if, as many have argued, there is a causal relation between consumer society and the weakening of shared governance, what changes can Americans make in how we think, and what can we salvage, foster, and create toward building and renewing a shared institutional authority geared to ameliorate social ills? I attempt to answer these questions in what follows by suggesting changes that can be made in our beliefs, behaviors, and institutions in regards to the three aspects of the *"default" model of the self*: metaphysical dualism, individualism, and expressivism.

II. A Way Forward for the Self

i. Belief

In this section, with the hopeful consequence of creating more substantial unity in public social structures, a number of changes to deeply held beliefs about the self that would be beneficial for our mental health, and make possible an understanding of our position in nature and history that is an alternative to the *"default" model of the self* shall be outlined. Although America is historically predominantly an individualist country (abstract, economic, and political individualism), there are numerous ways to understand the relation between the individual and the community. I suggest we put the current model of an individualist self into the communitarian context described in Chapter 2 through conceptualizing of psychological values and civic conditions as intrinsically social. This outwardly oriented model of the self propels a broader social orientation in citizens wherein general social issues become more important than, or more integrated with, particular personal interests. The individualist shift towards identity politics (i.e., ideologically fixed minority or special interests political groups whose social agenda is focused solely on the livelihood of one particular demographic) in the last 50 years has had a detrimental effect on the broader unity necessary for the public to apply requisite pressure on governing bodies.[4] Conceptualizing ourselves as members of larger communities first and foremost is a key step in strengthening the public voice. We have more in common than we think we do in an individualist framework; emphasizing uniqueness to the detriment of commonality has diluted the power of the greater body of citizens.

To demonstrate the ontological mistake of metaphysical dualism we need a broad set of educational programs that emphasize and clarify the scientific achievements of the last 50 years, which suggest the mind and brain are evolved elements of the species *Homo sapiens*, a mammal among other mammals within the natural world. Metaphysical dualism is an ontological mistake insofar as there is no evidence that the universe is made up of two substances; on the contrary, the evidence lies with the monist ontological position and specifically metaphysical materialism. This is not to say that we ought to devalue the *seemingly* non-physical mental sphere, rather, we must understand that the mental sphere is real in that we have subjective states, but it is not a separate substance that may transcend death, the mind is intrinsically tied to the physical material of which we are constituted. Explanations in terms of the tangible that do not invoke supernatural entities, that is, scientific naturalism, have developed greatly and can now offer reasonable models for what we are at a deep ontological level. Metaphysical dualism, as argued in Chapter 1, may be an evolutionary adaptation, but humans have the ability to understand that there are real phenomena outside our perceptual and cognitive limitations. Just as we cannot see ultraviolet rays, we are aware of their effects and therefore know they exist, the fact that we think we are dual creatures of body and soul should not overshadow what the scientific method suggests, namely that we are fundamentally embodied physical mindbrains. Positioning ourselves within the natural world puts the responsibility on us to make the most of this life and to have empathy for other members of our species (not to mention other species). If we are material creatures molded by evolution, and life is a precarious stage in the universe, then it is our responsibility to each other to structure our society toward ameliorating the quality of life for, at the least, all *Homo sapiens.* We need to broaden our scientific understanding of our relation to nature in terms of the monist mindbrain to change our broad and subtle behaviors influenced by the dead philosophical paradigm of metaphysical dualism.[5]

ii. Behavior

This section highlights changes in our behaviors that would be beneficial for more substantial unity in public social structures. The most important action toward this goal for individuals in a consumer society is to foster and create community organizations that are not based around the consumption of goods. For example, supporting extant public institutions like public libraries, public squares, public transportation, public parks, and public neighborhood festivals, is beneficial inasmuch as it demonstrates the worth of shared institutions and their ability to foster community.[6] Across the country, much of our shared infrastructure is suffering due to a depletion of public funds, or the redirection of public funds to institutions that serve private interests, for example, the city of Chicago's Tax Increment Financing program.[7] This depletion must be reversed through pressure on municipal, state, and federal institutions to support public infrastructure. At the same time it is necessary to boost self-generated do-it-yourself efforts at creating and fostering public institutions, like volunteer beach clean-ups, for example. The more we experience the vitality and positive effects of public institutions, the more likely we are to understand ourselves as a community. The more unity we feel in action, the more likely we are to respond to general discontent with public services by pressuring our democratically elected bodies at all levels of government to do their job of representing their whole constituency.

In terms of changing our behaviors in regards to expressivism in art, we have a trickier mandate in fostering art that fulfills social purposes while retaining vitality. I suggest we set the values of expressivism against a context where the purpose of art is shared emotional and intellectual bonds around the nature of the human condition. The conceptualization of art as simply an outpouring of emotions, or therapeutic catharsis misses out on the way in which art serves as a means for articulating emotional—and rational—visions of meaning as they pertain to universal human experiences. It is not detrimental to society that we see others and ourselves as possessing an inner space, but it is baleful to shortchange that space as simply storage for personal emotions that are mainly manifested in inwardly-oriented art objects that do not serve social purposes. Expression itself is not so special; rather, the fact that others can understand expression is what makes it so valuable. The latter element of expression deserves just as much recognition as the act of expression itself since it embeds us further into our social communities and strengthens our complex emotional bonds with others toward the strengthening of our commonalities and a greater public unity.

iii. Institutions—Art, Activism, and the Public Sphere[8]

Our ultimate goal in shifting away from the values and meaning derived from consumer society in the political context should be to take back the parts of government that no longer serve the purpose of representative shared governance. This is most pressing in elements of public services that should not have profit as their main motive, namely, the media (as a functioning media is necessary for a functioning democracy; see Chapter 5), education (as a "good" education cannot be measured by the profit of a given school), cultural events, and health care. The corporate concept of efficiency—that is, the relation between money in to money out—should not determine how particular elements of the public sector are framed because some things are good in themselves or serve more abstract goals like pluralism or social cohesion—for example, cultural events and community meetings—and some things are long-term investments or have social benefits, for example, education, libraries, cultural events, and health care.

Within a consumer society, in what ways can citizens effect a change in domestic policy in these areas? Commonly discussed platforms for citizens to organize toward enacting changes in domestic policy in the public sphere are on the Internet or, through art.

Some critics claim the Internet is the most promising platform for effective communication and organization between citizens such that the loss of physical public space (e.g., parking lots instead of parks) may be made up for by virtual public space.[9] Two questions seem pertinent here: can a private company create public space?[10] And are virtual relationships enough to unite the public? A recent argument states that it was the virtual public spaces of social media (e.g., Facebook and Twitter) that made the Arab Spring possible.[11] The Internet is a significantly different form of public space for a host of reasons, one of them being the sovereignty of the individual in virtual space; true public space is not under any single citizen's absolute control. Certainly, the successful revolutions in the collectivist countries Egypt and Tunisia in 2011 demonstrate the power of citizens to effect social change when they have public spaces and forums to congregate with a unified voice about a particular subject. Egyptians and Tunisians had access to communication across social network spaces as well as in the Middle Eastern public space of the street, the nargilah café, and the mosque. When curfews were imposed, landline and cellular telephones were used, when telephone lines were cut, the Internet was used, and when those were cut too, people went out into the street to agreed-upon or well-known meeting points (e.g., Tahrir square in Cairo). That is, virtual public space is just another forum for communication between citizens; it does not make up for the loss of physical public space, because ultimately human communication, certainly at crisis levels, requires physical space. It is this possibility—using the ultimate lever of power, namely the sheer volume of a population—that is taken away when physical public space is not available. This is not to say that America has the same level of devastating social ills that Egypt and Tunisia faced at the times of their uprisings, but the levers for enacting far smaller social changes also requires public space. What makes a gathering of citizens significant enough to effect change in governmental policy outside of the voting booth in case the voting process itself, or the legislative and executive branches, are not efficiently representing the needs of the constituencies? A recent American example of calls for non-revolutionary social change in domestic policy is the Occupy Wall Street group's protests at the federal government's bailout of Wall Street without provisions for structural change. This group based their 2011 campaign out of Zuccotti park at self-organized political gatherings and aired their grievances with placards and marches, while a similar Occupy group based in Chicago did not have access to public space in the downtown area and were unable to build similar effective long-term protest structures that may ultimately result in changes in domestic policy. Situations that make our shared life more important than our personal lives will arise at one point or another, for example, natural disasters, war, shortage of crucial resources, massive unemployment, or grave injustices. When these events arise, whether it is a consumer society or not, people will respond, and physical public space will be created if it is not already available.

A more egregious problem, argued in Adam Curtis' *Century of the Self* (2002), is that consumer society satisfies the needs of enough of the population that public resolve never reaches a point where political avenues to enact change become necessary. Technically, stability for a given government depends on satisfying the needs of its citizens. Consumer society itself was created to satisfy many human needs. Within consumer society, if you are in a position to take part, it is perfectly satisfactory at those particular levels of satisfaction. If you are not allowed to take part, you can get credit and take part anyways, although there are personal and societal consequences for this path, for example the sub-prime mortgage debacle of the late-aughts and the ever-declining national savings rate. Nevertheless, through credit and the creation of needs, consumer society can provide a bulwark against civil engagement by those whose position in society is not satisfactory. Whereas in the absence of consumption-centered modes of meaning to occupy and satisfy the citizens' psychological needs, these members of society may seek redress to make their position in society and society's relation to them more satisfactory.

In addition to the public sphere, the Internet, and public space, there are symbolic forms of activism that are effective in galvanizing and uniting the public voice. Art in the modern era (certainly since the French Revolution and previous to that to some extent) is understood to hold the possibility of articulating the public voice. For example, in the September 2009 edition of British music magazine *The Wire* there was an article on an international "political-aesthetic organization" that combines music and activism called Ultra Red (Fisher, 2008). They are part of a long tradition of leftist politics in modernist art enterprises, like the Situationist International (1957–1972). Their goal is political action that interrogates the aesthetic dimensions of political organization and produces public space. Art has a hallowed position in liberal post-enlightenment culture and is allowed certain political liberties—or takes certain political liberties by subterfuge. In addition, art speaks to the whole person; it is holistic communication at both the emotional and rational level. To be successful, social art must achieve a careful balance between message and aesthetics while avoiding the Scylla and Charybdis of being either emotionally barren or overly pedantic. An example of the powerful effects of art was Gustave Courbet's *Stonebreakers* of 1849, which served as a commentary on the plight of the lower classes in rapidly industrializing France at the time of the massive upheavals of thought wrought by the writings of Karl Marx on the social revolutions of 1848. Courbet's painting, as well as Eugene Delacroix's *Massacre of Chios* of 1824, painted as a protest at the failure of the French government to become involved in the Greek war for independence, were two of the many paintings in France's tumultuous nineteenth century that made current affairs palpable to the French public in such a way that the body of citizens were outraged enough to put pressure on governing bodies. More recently, art maintains the possibility of enacting widespread awareness and change, for example, the Mothers of the Plazo de Mayo movement in Argentina (1977–2006) that began as a small public protest by mothers of those "disappeared" during the country's dirty war (1976–1983), whose marches gave rise to an art movement in which the white scarves worn by the bereaved mothers served as a visual symbol of national protest. In addition, Chilean contemporary artist Alfredo Jaar (b. 1956) has an ever-growing oeuvre of sociopolitical art including an extended project on the Rwandan genocide and a performance project on both sides of the Mexican-American border that dramatized this locus of neoliberal globalization. Art as a powerful symbolic and emotional lever for dissent and clarity can serve as the incisive conscience of the public in times of peace and must not give up this function and duty for the facile pleasures of expressivism.

A more nefarious way of understanding consumer society in America is that elected government is not the most powerful element in society and that the political and economic order is in the hands of an unelected set of disparate organizations. If this is the case, what modes of agency remain available to citizens?

III. Skepticism and Agency in Consumer Society[12]

In the age of Neoliberalism—when a handful of private interests control as much as they can of social life in order to maximize personal profit—there is reason to believe governmental foreign and domestic policy is in the hands of private corporations and the electoral process itself is structured so that candidates can only run if they are sponsored by powerful elements of the private sector.[13] Furthermore, the policies of the two political parties are increasingly defined solely by the industries that sponsor them, rather than the citizens they are elected to represent. Although the rhetoric in Washington D.C. pays lip service to representative democracy and freedom (i.e., the core American values), there are a large, and rapidly increasing, number of indications that suggest federal and state governing bodies disproportionately represent private corporate interests to the detriment of the public interest; this becomes especially obvious in times of crisis.[14] But the problem is not simply top-down. In terms of representative democracy as embodied in the right to vote, during the late-twentieth century, individualist citizens can be characterized as voting mainly to protect their personal interests without sufficient concern for the greater public good. The low-income segments of American society largely do not vote for both technical reasons, like not having a stable address, and structural reasons such as, a lack of education and access to reliable information.[15] In this scheme, the right to vote is not successful enough in reflecting the political will of a representative proportion of the population. As of 2010, economic equality in America has reached a grave level of disproportion: a full 40 percent of production is in the speculative financial sector, correlatively, 43 percent of financial wealth is held by the top 1 percent, and 25 percent of GDP goes to the top 1 percent of the population (approximately 100,000 people) (Stiglitz, 2010). The current unemployment rate of 10–18 percent, artificially avoided for decades through speculative bubbles (savings and loan, real estate, stock market), may be the new normalcy since there are few possibilities for speculative bubbles or new industries at this point. Subsequently, the consequences of economic downturn become clearly noticeable in the depletion of public programs, for example, the discontinuation of unemployment benefits, by a federal government withered by years of cuts made despite their negative effects on shared public institutions.

These political and economic realities can be debilitating to the will of citizens. But surely representative democracy is not as dead in America as it is in nations with autocratic political systems? Does the infrastructure of representative democracy hold the possibility of transforming government into a more representative social institution, again?[16] Or, are the two factors I have discussed: the current structure of authority in private hands, and the infrastructure of electoral politics, insurmountable obstacles for the goal of shared governance geared toward the public good of all citizens?

These macroscopic problems relate to the microscopic personal decisions we each make in structuring our lives based on our values and the meaning we give to our actions. As argued throughout the book, as social creatures many of our goals are largely concerned with identity, in the context of consumer society, these goals take the form of purchasing decisions and in turn can lead to distinct social groupings based on our *taste*. This state of affairs in America, for a number of reasons, has led to a thriving private sector and a starving public sector, which in turn has negative consequences for economic equality, national unity, an empathetic and balanced foreign policy, and our system of representative democracy. To rectify the situation as described, it is imperative to maintain and nurture a diverse range of non-commercial relations between people and spaces for these relations to take place. Consumer society is not conducive to non-commercial civic relations, whereas public institutions, family, and traditional social rituals always have been, and remain, integral in this respect. Although there is ample room for pessimism, recent events in the Arab Spring remind us that even in brutal regimes, the public, once it finds its voice, is the true life of the nation. Whereas the Arab Spring took place in the face of autocratic leaders, what is more important in America is developing effective levers to power and political authority in times of peace. This work is, arguably, half finished: America has a wide range of extant public institutions. These institutions were created throughout its history and most notably during the New Deal. We must guard and foster these institutions; we must find ways to rejuvenate what has been dismantled or syncretized during the congealing of consumer society. That is to say, consumer society is a social, political, economical, and, most importantly, ethical, form for structuring social and personal relations. It is not going anywhere in the future— nor should it, necessarily—the problems recounted in this conclusion are consequences of the relations between how we conceptualize ourselves and how that has been amplified at the macroscopic realm of society. It is at the level of the self that I have focused and for which I make the following concluding suggestions.

IV. Conclusion

A first step in transforming elements of the *"default" model of the self* that have negative consequences for the collective body of citizens, is conceptualizing ourselves not as individuals but as members of communities, not as disembodied spirits but as evolved mindbrains, and viewing our actions as expressions of, not our uniqueness, but rather our deep embeddedness in, and indebtedness to, society. Our communities—all the way from the local to the national—depend upon, and are molded by, the self. In America, the self has been perpetuated by, and itself has perpetuated, consumer society. The social relations this form of society breeds are not entirely conducive to successful representative democracy, nor do they help us fulfill some of our highest goals as civilized human beings: equality of resources, harmony, and liberty. It is for these reasons that the self is ground zero for how humans relate to each other and the world around them, and it is within the locus of the self that important changes need to occur so as detrimental social and cultural processes may be diminished and, in time, eradicated. Changes in the way we each give value and meaning to our actions, if implemented, would be amplified to constitute a different form of society, a different form of relating, and ultimately, a different form of living.

Notes

1 The ruling, *Citizens United v. Federal Election Commission*, No. 08–205, overruled two precedents: *Austin v. Michigan Chamber of Commerce*, a 1990 decision that upheld restrictions on corporate spending to support or oppose political candidates, and *McConnell v. Federal Election Commission*, a 2003 decision that upheld the part of the *Bipartisan Campaign Reform Act of 2002* that restricted campaign spending by corporations and unions. (Liptak, 2010). Justices, 5–4, Reject Corporate Spending Limit. New York Times. Published: January 21, 2010.

2 See Robert Reich's (2007) analysis of this process in *Supercapitalism*. Reich emphasizes the related problems of the inordinate amount of money and time spent on policy matters in courts of law and lobbying that would be more appropriately dealt with by governmental regulation. Furthermore, he explains that our goal in ending corruption in the current political system should be to root out systemic rot in areas of power where corporate proxies have taken up position, specifically, lobby groups with access to members of legislative bodies and members of private corporations who hold seats on the cabinet of the executive branch.

3 Not to mention the effect that this organization of power has on foreign policy.

4 See Taylor's (1989) discussion of the impossibility of protest after identity politics.

5 For a start see the work of Columbia College Chicago LAS Research Group in Mind, Science, and Culture, of which I am a member, at www.mindscienceculture.com.

6 Cf. Putnam, R. (2000). *Bowling Alone: The collapse and revival of American community*. New York: Simon & Schuster.

7 See journalist Ben Joravsky's numerous exposés on this misappropriation of public funds in the pages of the *Chicago Reader*. Another notable article on this phenomenon is Matt Taibbi's Looting Main Street in *Rolling Stone* (March 31, 2010). On the national level, there are scores of these models that are benignly referred to as "private-public partnerships" (Klein, 2001; Schiller, 1989).

8 My understanding of the term public sphere is derived from Habermas, J. (1989). The Structural Transformation of the Public Sphere: An Inquiry into a category of Bourgeois Society. Cambridge, MA: The MIT Press.

9 See Boeder, P. (2005). Habermas' legacy: The future of the public sphere in a network society. *First Monday* 10 (9). Although see Fraser, N. (1990). Rethinking the public sphere: A contribution to the critique of actually existing democracy. *Social Text* 25/26. 56–80.

10 For example, *everyblock.com*, a Chicago-based private company that provides a platform for people to share news about their community with other members of the community. As of this writing it is still not for profit although it has been acquired by MSNBC. The founder of the company claims the public sector should provide services while private sector should provide products. In this case, public space is being conceptualized as a service.

11 For a more cautious analysis of the relation between the Arab Spring and social media, see Steve Coll's review in NYRB: (http://www.nybooks.com/articles/archives/2011/apr/07/internet-better-or-worse/), and Michael Teague's 2011 review in Al Jadid: (http://www.aljadid.com/content/new-media-and-arab-spring).

12 Much of this section was sparked by a lively conversation between the author, the economist Rojhat Avsar, and the social activist Tom Greif.

13 There is a range of literature that makes these claims, I simply refer you to one prolific writer, Noam Chomsky, see, for example, his *Profits over people: Neoliberalism and global order* (1999). New York, NY: Seven Stories Press. In which he claims neoliberalism undermines public institutions like health care and education while increasing inequality and reducing labor's share in income. Also see Schiller (1989).

14 Look no further than the federal government's pro-business, and simultaneous "leaving the powerless out to dry," response to the 2008 economic "collapse" documented in a number of books, including Nobel Prize winner Stiglitz (2010).

15 Not to mention the dismal voter turnout, which was about 40 percent in the 2010 national elections according to the United States election project (McDonald, 2010): http://elections.gmu.edu/index.html.

    Poor people do not vote for a number of reasons, including having weaker civic ties, being less mobilized by candidates, workday voting, felony disenfranchisement, the decrease in union fraternal civic associations that once motivated lower-income individuals, as well as a six-fold hike in the rate of incarceration over the past three decades (Soss & Jacobs, 2009).

16 Some critics may argue government in America was never representative, that the constitution itself was created to safeguard the landowning class (Greenwald, 2011). I concede there was never a time when the system of representative democracy worked perfectly, but insist that there were periods in the history of America when government represented a larger proportion of citizens than it does now. Therefore, although there was no perfect era in America—or any other country for that matter—there is the possibility of a more justly organized representative democracy, and that is what we ought to aim toward.

Bibliography

Introduction

Rochefort, R. (1995). *La Societé des consommateurs.* Paris: Editions Odile Jacob.

Chapter One

Aristotle. (1961). W.D. Ross (Ed). *De Anima*. Oxford: Clarendon Press.

——— (1987). H. Lawson-Tancred (Ed). *De Anima*. New York, NY: Penguin Classics.

Aquinas, T. (1999). R. McInerny (Ed). *Thomas Aquinas: Selected writings*. New York, NY: Penguin Classics.

Baron-Cohen, S. (1995). First lessons in mind reading. *The Times Higher Education Supplement*, June 16. Retrieved on August 12, 2010 from http://www.timeshighereducation.co.uk/story.asp?storyCode=98714&sectioncode=26.

Barrett, J. (2004). *Why would anyone believe in God?* Walnut Creek, CA: AltaMira Press.

Bering, J. (2002). The existential theory of mind. *Review of General Psychology*, 6(1), 3–24.

Bloom, P. (2004). *Descartes' baby*. New York, NY: Basic Books.

Damasio, A. (2011). *Self comes to mind*. New York, NY: Pantheon Press.

Dennett, D. (1987). *The intentional stance*. Cambridge, MA: The MIT Press.

Descartes, R. (1996). *Meditations on first philosophy*, translated by J. Cottingham. Cambridge, UK: Cambridge University Press.

Foley, M.P. (Ed.) (2007). *Confessions of St Augustine*, translated by F. J. Sheed. Indianapolis, IN: Hackett Publishing Company.

Gabriel, R. (2009). *The mind and the soul, paper*. Retrieved from mindscienceculture.com.

Gazzaniga, M. (1998). *The mind's past*. Berkeley, CA: University of California Press.

Gazzaninga, M.S. (1999). The interpreter within: The glue of conscious experience. *Cerebrum* 1(1), 68–78.

Heider, F., & Simmel, M. (1944). An experimental study of apparent behavior. *American Journal of Psychology*, 57, 243–259.

Honderich, T. (2004). *On consciousness*. Edinburgh, UK: Edinburgh University Press.

Humphrey, N. (1984). *Consciousness regained*. Oxford: Oxford University Press.

——— (1994). Reflections on consciousness. *The Psychologist*, 7, 259.

Klein, S.B., Rozendal, K., & Cosmides, L. (2002). A social-cognitive neuroscience analysis of the self. *Social Cognition*, 20, 105–135.

Leslie, A.M. (1987). Pretense and representation: The origins of "Theory of Mind". *Psychological Review*, 94(4), 412–426.

Lowe, E.J. (1993). The mind matters: Consciousness and choice in a quantum world. *Philosophical Books*, 34(1), 33–34.

Martin, R., & Barresi, J. (2006). *The rise and fall of soul and self*. New York, NY: Columbia University Press.

McComb, K., Baker, L., & Moss, C. (2005). African elephants show high levels of interest in the skulls and ivory of their own species. *Biology Letters*, 2, 26–28.

Moss, C. (1988). *Elephant memories*. USA: William Morow and Company, Inc.

Piaget, J. (1926). *The child's conception of the world*. London: Routledge & Kegan Paul.

Plato. (1993). C. Rowe (Ed). *Phaedo*. Cambridge: Cambridge University Press.

Popper & Eccles. (1977). *The self and its brain: An argument for interactionism*. United Kingdom: Springer.

Porter, R. (2003). *Flesh in the age of reason*. New York, NY: W.W. Norton and company.

Ryle, G. (1949). *The concept of mind*. London: Hutchinson.

Smith, J.D., Shields, W.E., Allendoerfer, K., & Washburn, W.A., (1998). Memory monitoring by animals and humans. *Journal of Experimental Psychology: General* 127(3), 227–250.

Spelke, E. (1998). Nativism, empiricism and the origins of knowledge. *Infant Behavior and Development*, 21, 181–200.

Tremlin, T. (2006). Minds and Gods. Oxford: Oxford University Press.

Wahrman, D. (2004). *The making of the modern self: Identity and culture in eighteenth-century England*. New Haven, CT: Yale University Press.

Wellman, H.M. (1990). *The child's theory of mind*. Cambridge, MA: The MIT Press.

Wellman, H. & Bartsch, K. (1988). Young children's reasoning about beliefs. *Cognition*, 30, 239–277.

Chapter Two

Avineri, S. & de-Shalit, A. (1992). *Communitarianism and individualism*. Oxford: Oxford University Press.

De Tocqueville, A. (2000). *Democracy in America*. Chicago, IL: The University of Chicago Press.

Etzioni, A. (1998). *The new golden rule: Community and morality in a democratic society*. New York, NY: Basic Books.

Flathman, R. (1998). *Reflections of a would-be anarchist: Ideals and institutions of liberalism*. Minneapolis, MN: University of Minnesota Press.

Hartz, L. (1955). *The liberal tradition in America: An interpretation of American political thought since the revolution*. New York, NY: Harcourt, Brace & World.

Haskell, T.L. (2000). Taking exception to exceptionalism. *Reviews in American History*, 28(1), March, 151–166.

Hobbes, T. (1651, 2010). I. Shapiro (Ed). *Leviathan: Or the matter, forme, and power of a commonwealth ecclesiasticall and civill*. New Haven, CT: Yale University Press.

Locke, J. (1690, 1980). C. B. Macpherson (Ed). *Second treatise of government*. Indianapolis, IN: Hackett.

Lipsitz, G. (1998). S. Strasser, C. McGovern & M. Judt (Eds). *Consumer spending as state project: Yesterday's solutions and today's problems in getting and spending: European and American consumer societies in the twentieth century*, Washington DC: Cambridge University Press, 136–140.

MacPherson, C.B. (1962). *The political theory of possessive individualism: From hobbes to locke*. Oxford: Clarendon Press.

Mill, J.S. (1859, 2002). *On liberty*. Mineola, NY: Dover Publications.

Sandel, M. (1992). *Liberalism and the limits of justice*. Cambridge: Cambridge University Press.

Schudson, M. (1998). *The good citizen*. New York, NY: Free Press.

Taylor, C. (1992). *Multiculturalism and the politics of recognition*. Princeton, NJ: Princeton University Press.

Wiebe, R.H. (1992). *Self-rule: A cultural history of American democracy*. Chicago and London: University of Chicago Press.

Chapter Three

Arnold, M. (1868). Below the surface-stream. First published in St. Paul and Protestantism II, *Cornhill Magazine*, November.

Bellah, R.N., Madsen, R., Sullivan, W.M., Swidler, A., & Tipton, S.M. (1996). *Habits of the heart: Individualism and commitment in American life*. Berkeley, CA: University of California Press.

Berlin, I. (2001). *The roots of romanticism*, edited by H. Hardy. Princeton, NJ: Princeton University Press.

Bourdieu, P. (1984). *Distinction: A social critique of the judgment of taste*. London: Routledge and Kegan Paul.

Campbell, C. (1987). *The romantic ethic and the spirit of modern consumerism*. Oxford: Blackwell.

Foucault, M. (1993). About the beginning of the hermeneutics of the self: Two lectures at Dartmouth. *Political Theory*, 21(2), 198–227.

Freud, S. (1916). *Introductory lectures on psychoanalysis*. Leipzig-Vienna: Hugo Heller.

Gans, H. (1974). *Popular culture and high culture*. New York, NY: Basic Books.

Guignon, C.B. (2004). *On being authentic*. London: Routledge.

Janov, A. (1970). *The primal scream*. New York, NY: Dell.

Lasch, C. (1979). *The culture of narcissism: American life in an age of diminishing expectations*. New York, NY: W.W. Norton and Company.

Rousseau, J-J. (1782, 1953). *The confessions*. New York, NY: Penguin Classics.

Rieff, P. (1959). *Freud: The mind of the moralist*. Chicago, IL: University of Chicago Press.

——— (1968). *The triumph of the therapeutic: Uses of faith after Freud*. Chicago, IL: University of Chicago Press.

Taylor, C. (1989). *Sources of the self: The making of modern identity*. Cambridge, MA: Harvard University Press.

——— (1991). *The ethics of authenticity*. Cambridge, MA: Harvard University Press.

Trilling, L. (1972). *Sincerity and authenticity*. London: Oxford University Press.

Whitman, W. (1885, 2000). *Leaves of grass*. New York, NY: New American Library.

Whyte, L.L. (1960). *The unconscious before Freud*. New York, NY: Basic Books.

Chapter Four

Barthes, R. (1972). *Mythologies*. Paris: Seuil.

Bell, D. (1976). *The cultural contradictions of capitalism*. New York, NY: Basic Books.

Bellah, R.N., Madsen, R., Sullivan, W.M., Swidler, A., & Tipton, S.M. (1996). *Habits of the heart: Individualism and commitment in American life*. Berkeley, CA: University of California Press.

Bourdieu, P. (1984). *Distinction: A social critique of the judgment of taste*. London: Routledge and Kegan Paul.

Breen, T.H. (2004). *Marketplace of revolution: How consumer politics shaped American independence*. New York, NY: Oxford University Press.

Chomsky, N. (1999). *Profit over people: Neoliberalism and global order*. USA: Seven Stories Press.

Cohen, L. (2003). *A consumers' republic: The politics of mass consumption in postwar America*. New York, NY: Knopf press.

Cross, G. (2001). *An all consuming century: Why commercialism won in modern America*. New York, NY: Columbia University Press.

De Vries, J. (2008). *The Industrious revolution: Consumer behavior and the household economy, 1650 to the present*. New York, NY: Cambridge University Press.

Etzioni, A. (1998). *The new golden rule: Community and morality in a democratic society*. New York, NY: Basic Books.

Ewen, S. (1988). *All consuming images: The politics of style in contemporary culture*. New York, NY: Basic Books.

——— (1976). *Captains of consciousness: Advertising and the social roots of the consumer culture*. New York, NY: McGraw-Hill.

Ewen, S. & Ewen, E. (1992). *Channels of desire: Mass images and the shaping of American consciousness*. Mineola, MN: University of Minnesota Press.

Fox, R. & Lears. J. (1983). *The culture of consumption: Critical essays in American history, 1880–1980*. New York, NY: Pantheon Books.

Galbraith, J.K. & Salinger, N. (1990). *Almost everyone's guide to economics*. New York, NY: Penguin's Books.

Galbraith, J.K. (1958). *The Affluent society*, 40th anniversary edition. New York, NY: Mariner Books.

Giddens, A. (1991). *Modernity and self-Identity: Self and society in the late modern age*. Stanford, CA: Stanford University Press.

Gladwell, M. (1997). The coolhunt. *The New Yorker*, March 17. 78–88.

Glickman, L. B. (1999). *Consumer Society in American History: A Reader*. Ithaca, NY & London: Cornell University Press.

Harvey, D. (1989). *The condition of postmodernity: An enquiry into the origins of cultural change*. Oxford: Blackwell Publishers.

Hirsch, F. (1976). *Social limits to growth*. Cambridge, MA: Harvard University Press.

Illinois General Assembly (1975). *Redlining: Discrimination in residential mortgage loans*. Chicago, IL: Legislative Investigating Commission.

Jansson, A. (2001). *Image culture: Media, consumption & everyday life in reflexive modernity*. Goteborgs: Unversitet Acta Univ.

Klein, N. (2001). *No logo*. New York, NY: Picador.

Krugman, P. (1997). *The age of diminished expectations: U.S. economic policy in the 1990s*, 3rd ed. Cambridge, M: The MIT Press.

Leach, W.R. (1994). *Land of desire: Merchants, power, and the rise of a new American culture*. New York, NY: Vintage.

Lears, J. (1994). *No place of grace: antimodernism and the transformation of American culture, 1880–1920*. Chicago, IL: University of Chicago Press.

——— (1995). *Fables of abundance: a cultural history of advertising in America*. New York, NY: Basic Books.

Leiss, W., Kline, S., Jhally, S. & Boterill, J. (2005). *Social communication in advertising: Consumption in the mediated marketplace*, third ed. New York, NY: Routledge.

Lilla, M. (2010). The tea party jacobins. *The New York Times Review of Books*, 57 (9), May 27.

Lury, C. (1996). *Consumer culture*. Rutgers, NJ: Rutgers University Press.

Lynes, J.R. (1949). *The tastemakers*. New York, NY: Grosset and Dunlap.

Martin, B. (1981). *Sociology of contemporary cultural change*. Oxford: Blackwell.

McCracken, G. (1988). *Culture and consumption: New approaches to the symbolic character of consumer goods and activities*. Bloomington, IN: Indiana University Press.

McKendrick, N., Brewer, J., & Plumb, J.H. (1982). *The birth of a consumer society: The commercialization of eighteenth century England*. London: Europa Publications.

Norton, A. (1993). *Republic of signs: Liberal theory and American popular culture*. Chicago: The University of Chicago Press.

Potter, A. & Heath, J. (2004). *The rebel sell*. Canada: Harper Collins.

Reich, R. (2007). *Supercapitalism*. New York, NY: Knopf Press.

Schudson, M. (1998). *The good citizen*. New York, NY: Free Press.

Sennett, R. (1978). *The fall of public man – on the social psychology of capitalism*. New York: Vintage Books/Random House.

Tiersten, L. (2001). *Marianne in the marketplace: Envisioning consumer society in fin-de-siècle France*. Berkeley, CA: University of California Press.

Wernick, A. (1992). *Promotional culture: Advertising, ideology and symbolic expression*. Thousand Oaks, CA: Sage.

Veblen, T. (1899). *The theory of the leisure class*. London: MacMillan.

Zinn, H. (2009). *The Zinn reader*. New York, NY: Seven Stories Press.

Zola, E. (1883). *Au bonheur des dames*. Paris: Charpentier.

Chapter Five

Appadurai, A. (Ed.) (1986). *The social life of things: Commodities in cultural perspective.* Cambridge: Cambridge University Press.

Bagdikian, B.H. (1997). *The media monopoly.* New York, NY: Beacon Press.

Barthes, R. (1972). *Mythologies.* Paris: Seuil.

Bourdieu, P. (1984). *Distinction: A social critique of the judgment of taste.* London: Routledge and Kegan Paul.

Chandler, D. (2004). *Semiotics: The basics.* London: Routledge.

Cohen, L. (2003). *A consumers' republic: The politics of mass consumption in postwar America.* New York, NY: Knopf Press.

Curti, M. (1967). The changing concept of human nature in the literature of American advertising. *Business History Review*, 41, 335–357.

Douglas, M., & Isherwood, B. (1996). *The world of goods: Towards an anthropology of consumption.* London: Routledge.

Hall, S. (1980). Encoding and decoding in the television discourse. In S. Hall (Ed). *Culture, media, language: Working papers in cultural studies.* London: Hutchinson.

Henry, J. (1963). *Culture against man.* New York, NY: Vintage books.

Jhally, S. (1987). *The codes of advertising.* New York, NY: St. Martin's Press.

Lears, J. (1994). *No place of grace: Antimodernism and the transformation of American culture, 1880–1920.* Chicago, IL: University of Chicago Press.

—— (1995). *Fables of abundance: A cultural history of advertising in America.* New York, NY: Basic Books.

Leiss, W. (1976). *The limits of satisfaction.* Toronto and Buffalo: University of Toronto Press.

Leiss, W., Kline, S., Jhally, S. & Boterill, J. (2005). *Social communication in advertising: Consumption in the mediated marketplace*, third ed. New York, NY: Routledge.

Leach, E. (1989). Claude Lévi-Strauss. Chicago, IL: University of Chicago Press.

Leach, W.R. (1994). *Land of desire: Merchants, power, and the rise of a new American culture.* New York, NY: Vintage.

Lévi-Strauss, C. (1963, 1967). *Structural anthropology*, translated by C. Jacobson & B.G. Schoepf. New York, NY: Doubleday Anchor Books.

Langholz Leymore, V. (1975). *Hidden myth.* London: Heinemann.

Lucas, D.B & Britt, S. H. (1950). *Advertising psychology and research: An introductory book.* New York, NY: McGraw-Hill Book Company.

Marchand, R. (1986). *Advertising the American dream: Making way for modernity, 1920 – 1940.* Berkeley, CA: University of California Press.

McAllister, M.P. (1996). *The commercialization of American culture: New advertising, control and democracy.* Thousand Oaks, CA: Sage.

McChesney, R.W. (2002). *Rich media, poor democracy.* New York, NY: New Press.

McChesney, R.W. & Nichols, J. (2002). *Our media, not theirs.* Canada: Seven Stories Press.

McChesney, R.W. & Scott, B. (2004). *Our unfree press: 100 years of radical media criticism.* United States: New Press.

Meyers, W. (1984). *The image makers: Secrets of successful advertising.* New York, NY: Papermac.

O'Barr, W.M. (2010). Advertising and media. *Advertising & Society Review, 11 (1).*

Pease, O. (1958). *The responsibilities of American advertising: Private control and public influence, 1920–1940.* New Haven, CT: Yale University Press.

Pope, D. (1983). *The making of modern advertising.* New York, NY: Basic Books.

Rapaille, C. (2006). *The culture code: An ingenious way to understand why people around the world live and buy as they do.* New York, NY: Broadway.

Schrank, J. (1979). *Snap, crackle, popular taste.* New York, NY: Dell.

Schudson, M. (1984). *Advertising, the uneasy persuasion: It's dubious impact on American society.* New York, NY: Basic Books.

Sahlins, M. (1976). *Culture and practical reason.* Chicago, IL: University of Chicago Press.

Sampson, S. (1974). *A history of advertising from the earliest times.* London: Chatto and Windus.

Simpson, C. (1994). *The science of coercion: Communication research and psychological warfare 1945–1960.* Oxford: Oxford University Press.

Story, L. (2007). Anywhere the eye can see, it's likely to see an ad. *New York Times,* January 15.

Tungate, M. (2007). *Adland: A global history of advertising.* New York, NY: Kogan Page Limited.

Walker, R. (2008). *Buying in: The secret dialogue between what we buy and who we are.* New York, NY: Random House.

Williamson, J. (1994). *Decoding advertisements: Ideology and meaning in advertising.* London: Marion Boyars.

Chapter Six

Abaza, M. (2001). Shopping malls, consumer culture and the reshaping of public space in Egypt. *Theory, Culture, & Society,* 18, 97–122.

——— (2006). *Changing consumer cultures of modern Egypt: Cairo's urban reshaping.* Leiden and Boston: Brill and American University in Cairo Press.

de Grazia, V. (1998). Changing consumption regimes in Europe, 1930–70, comparative perspectives on the distribution problem. In S. Strasser, C. McGovern, & M. Judt. (Eds). *Getting and spending: Comparative perspectives on consumer culture.* Cambridge: German Historical Institute and Cambridge University Press.

De Mooij, M. (2004). *Consumer behavior and culture. consequences for global marketing and advertising.* Thousand Oaks, CA: Sage.

——— (2005). *Global marketing and advertising, understanding cultural paradoxes,* second edition. Thousand Oaks, CA: Sage.

Freeman, L., Diaz, A.-C,. Beardi, C., & Webster, N.C. (2000). Decade in review. *Advertising age,* 71(11), S14.

Geertz, C. (1973). Thick description: toward an interpretive theory of culture, (from his book *The interpretation of cultures: selected essays* (pp. 3–30). New-York: Basic Books.). In Lincoln, Y.S., & Denzin, N.K. (Eds). Turning points in qualitative research (pp. 143–159). Walnut Creek, CA: Altamira.

Han, S. & Shavitt, S. (1994). Persuasion and culture: Advertising appeals in individualistic and collectivistic societies. *Journal of Experimental Social Psychology*, 30, 326–350.

Hofstede, G. (1983). National cultures in four dimensions: A research-based theory of cultural differences among nations. *International Studies of Management & Organization*, 13(1/2), Cross-Cultural Management: II. Empirical Studies (Spring–Summer), 46–74.

Holt, D.B. (1998). Does cultural capital structure American consumption. *Journal of Consumer Research*, 25 (1), 1–25.

Hopwood, D. (1982). *Egypt: Politics and society 1945–1981*. London: George Allen and Unwin.

Hui, C.H. & Triandis, H.C. (1985). Measurement in cross-cultural psychology: A review and comparison of strategies. *Journal of Cross-Cultural Psychology*, 16, 131–152.

Kroen, S. (2004). Le magie des objects, le plan Marshall et l'instauration d'une democratie de consommateurs. In A. Chatriot, M-E. Chessel, & M. Hilton (Eds.), *Au nom du consommateur: Consommation et politique in Europe et aux Etats-Unis au XXe siecle*. Paris: Editions la Decouverte.

Kuisel, R.F. (1993). *Seducing the french: The dilemma of Americanization*. Berkeley, CA: University of California Press.

Leiss, W., Kline, S., Jhally, S. & Botterill, J. (2005). *Social communication in advertising: Consumption in the mediated marketplace*, third edition. New York, NY: Routledge press.

Mitchell, T. (1999). *Dreamland: The neoliberalism of your desires*. Middle East Report (Spring), 28–33.

McClay, W.H. (1994). *The masterless: Self & society in modern America*. Chapel Hill, NC: University of North Carolina Press.

Rochefort, R. (1995). *La Societé des consommateurs*. Paris: Editions Odile Jacob.

Rodenbeck, M. (1999). *Cairo, the city victorious*. Cairo: The American University Press.

Rokeach, M. (1973). *The nature of human values*. New York, NY: Free Press.

Rugh, A.B. (1984). *Family in contemporary Egypt*. Syracuse, NY: Syracuse University Press.

Rutherford, B.K. (2008). *Egypt after mubarak: Liberalism, islam, and democracy in the Arab world*. USA: Princeton University Press.

Said, E. (1979). *Orientalism*. New York, NY: Vintage Books.

Stearns. P. (2001). *Consumerism in world history: The global transformation of desire*. London: Routledge.

Tiersten, L. (2001). *Marianne in the marketplace: Envisioning consumer society in fin-de-siècle France*. Berkeley, CA: University of California Press.

Triandis, H.C., Bontempo, R., Villareal, M.J., Asai, M. & Lucca, N. (1988). Individualism and collectivism: Cross-cultural perspectives on self-ingroup relationships. *Journal of Personality and Social Psychology*, 54, 323–338.

Triandis, H.C. (1989). The self and social behavior in differing cultural contexts. *Psychological Review*, 96(3), 506–520.

Williams, R. (1982). *Dream worlds: Mass consumption in late nineteenth-century France*. Berkeley, CA: University of California Press.

Shame and Islam. *Doctor Sanity*. Retrieved on May 29, 2011 from http://drsanity.blogspot.com/2005/08/shame-arab-psyche-and-islam.html.

Conclusion

Boeder, P. (2005). Habermas' legacy: The future of the public sphere in a network society. *First Monday*, 10(9).

Chomsky, N. (1999). *Profits over people: Neoliberalism and global order*. New York, NY: Seven Stories Press.

Coll, S. (2011). The internet: For better or worse. *New York Review of Books*, 58 (6) April 7.

Curtis, A., Dir. (2002). *Century of the self*. BBC Four, Film.

Fisher, M. (2008). Ultra-red. *Wire*, September, 28–33.

Fraser, N. (1990). Rethinking the public sphere: A contribution to the critique of actually existing democracy. *Social Text*, 25/26, 56–0.

Greenwald, G. (2011). *With liberty and justice for some*. New York, NY: Metropolitan Books.

Habermas, J. (1989). *The structural transformation of the public sphere: An inquiry into a category of bourgeois society*. Cambridge, MA: The MIT Press.

Klein, N. (2001). *No logo*. New York, NY: Picador.

Liptak, A. (2010). Justices, 5–4, reject corporate spending limit. *New York Times*, January 21.

Putnam, R. (2000). *Bowling alone: The collapse and revival of American community*. New York: Simon & Schuster.

Reich. R. (2007). *Supercapitalism*. New York, NY: Knopf Press.

Schiller, H.I. (1989). *Culture, Inc.: the corporate takeover of public expression*. New York, NY: Oxford University Press.

Soss, J. & Jacobs, L.R. (2009). The place of inequality: Non-participation in the American polity. *Political Science Quarterly*, 124(1), 95–125.

Stiglitz, J.E. (2010). *Freefall: America, free markets, and the sinking of the world economy*. New York, NY: W.W. Norton and company.

Taibbi, M. (2010). Looting main street. *Rolling Stone*, March 31.

Taylor, C. (1989). *Sources of the self: The making of modern identity*. Cambridge, MA: Harvard University Press.

Teague, M. (2011). New media and the Arab spring. *Al Jadid*. May 8.

McDonald, M. "2010 national vote". *United States Election Project*. Retrieved on August 18, 2011 from http://elections.gmu.edu/index.html.

Appendix

Representative examples of advertisements used in study:

Egypt

Figure 1: *Beymen* – Dualism (taken from *Flash*, November 2009).

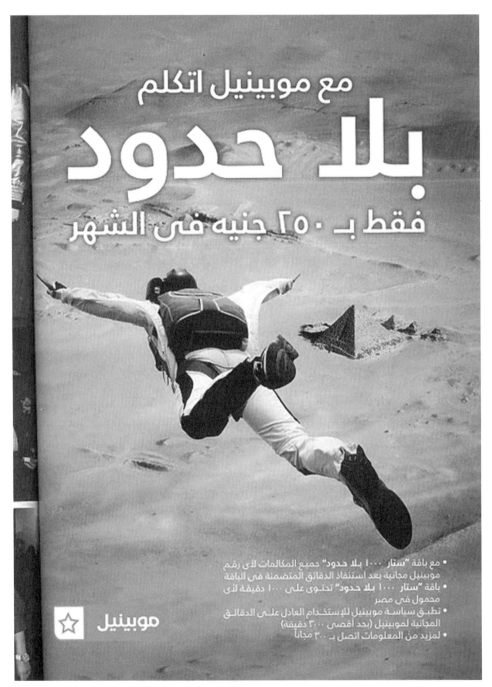

Figure 2: *Mobinil* – Expressivism (taken from *Flash*, December 2009).

Figure 3: *Glamour Jewelry* – Individualism (taken from *Flash*, September 2009).

French

Figure 4: *Faith Connexion* – Dualism (taken from *French Vogue*, August 2009).

Figure 5: *John Galliano* – Expressivism (taken from *Paris Match*, May 14–20 2009).

Figure 6: *Fruit and Form* – Individualism (taken from *French Gala,* June 15 2009).

America

Figure 7: *Juicy Couture* – Dualism (taken from *Vogue,* October 2009).

Figure 8: *Juicy Couture* – Expressivism (taken from *Vogue*, October 2009).

Figure 9: *Ray-Ban* – Individualism (taken from *GQ*, October 2009).

Index